D1487739

The Ultimate Beginner's Running Guide

THE ULTIMATE BEGINNER'S RUNNING GUIDE

THE KEY TO RUNNING INSPIRED

RYAN ROBERT

© 2012 by Ryan Robert. All rights reserved. Published by Ryan Robert. No part of this publication may be reproduced or distributed in any form or by any means, or stored in a database or retrieval system without the prior written permission of Ryan Robert.

The Author and publisher have used their best efforts in preparing this book and the document contained herein. However, the author and publisher make no warranties of any kind, express or implied, with regard to the informational content, documentation, or files contained in this book or in any accompanying media files such as CDs or DVDs, and specifically disclaim, without limitation, any implied warranties of merchantability and fitness for a particular purpose, with respect to program listings in the book, the techniques described in the book, and/or the use of files. In no event shall the author or publisher be responsible or liable for loss of profit, or any commercial damages, including, but not limited to, special incidental, consequential, or any other damages in connection with or arising out of furnishing, performance, or use of this book, program files, instruction, audio or video connected with this information.

Further, the author and publisher have used their best efforts to proof and confirm the content of the files, but you should proof and confirm information such as dates, measurements, and any other content for yourself. The author and publisher make no warranties of any kind, express or implied, with regard to that content or its accuracy.

ISBN-13: 978-1482046625
ISBN-10: 1482046628

The Ultimate Beginner's Running Guide: The Key to Running Inspired

TABLE OF CONTENTS

Chapter 8: Running Inspired   123

Chapter 9: Training Schedules   127

Introduction: Why Run?

What we call the beginning is often the end. And to make an end is to make a beginning. The end is where we start from.
--T.S. Eliot

Whatever the reasons are that we begin thinking about running, it begins, as Eliot reminds us, with an ending. We are ready to end some part of our lives that we don't like, and replace it with something healthy and gratifying.

To begin running is to truly begin building self confidence, to enjoy being outdoors with friends and fellow runners, or to be by ourselves for reflection and solitude.

There are many health-related reasons to run, which will be covered later in this introduction to reinforce the decision to begin running. But as runners just starting out, our first rationale should be very personal and specific. We may start exercising and running with a fairly superficial rationale: "I want to be able to fit into my wedding dress;" "the doctor said I need to start doing something good for myself;" "I want to shed those holiday pounds." Although these are great seeds of motivation, there will be times when we need *more* than simply, "I want to look better for my partner," or "Well, the doctor says I should, so I guess I will."

You will find that if you run consistently, all of the issues of weight, appearance, self-esteem, and physical and mental health come together in overall fitness. In the final analysis we will continue running, training, and maintaining a healthy lifestyle only by being gracefully selfish and doing what is good for our overall health, mind and body, and not for a specific event or someone else.

This book and the running schedules enclosed are aimed at helping beginner runners get started no matter their level of fitness, weight, age, or location.   One of the most wonderful things about running is that it can be embraced by virtually anyone, anywhere in the world.   Basic questions will be answered about preparing to run, footwear and gear, raising your level of fitness and intensity once you've begun, nutrition and weight loss, and common injuries.

Because the mental aspect of running is such an enormous part of the sport, at the end of each chapter is a short visualization exercise.   Visualization has been proven to stimulate the same areas of the brain as the actual exercise, but more importantly it helps us to overcome the initial problems of procrastination and lack of motivation.   For example, NBA players spend hours visualizing exactly how they will shoot a free throw—stepping up to the line, one, two, three dribbles of the ball, elbow forward, eyes focused . . . can you see it in your mind's eye?

Using the same techniques, we envision ourselves lacing up our running shoes, stepping out the door and breathing in the fresh air; then walking briskly toward the starting point of our run.   We feel good, with shoulders and upper body loose, and legs feeling strong and agile.

Another reason for the visualizations is to help us to remember how much we've accomplished as we continue to run, and how much has changed in our lives since we've started running. Running is essentially an extremely (wonderful) vicious cycle—the more we run the better runners we become; the better runners we become the more pride we take in ourselves, our nutrition and lifestyle; the more pride we have in ourselves the more we enjoy running and so become more motivated to run . . . After a few weeks or months it is very easy to take this progress for granted; we use visualization to remember how far we've come and how far we have to go.

This cycle of feeling good because you feel good actually has a very sound basis in the body's biochemical reaction to exercise and specifically to running—we can actually train our bodies to produce the chemicals to make us healthier and happier!

Perhaps you, too, have marveled at the "fanatics" who run in all kinds of weather and treat their training as if it were a religion. These runners don't necessarily possess special dedication pills, rare ambition genes, and are not particularly self-disciplined; but have found that running enacts the cycle of pleasure and gratification; offering the unique set of internal and external rewards that only running can provide.

As beginner runners we can become so caught up in the details of the sport and getting ready to exercise that we forget that all we really need are a pair of sneakers and some open ground to run across. The term running as a "sport" is used very loosely—running is also a hobby, a way to meditate, or a simple way to achieve goals without videos, programs, or expensive gym memberships. There are three major things to remember, which will be repeated throughout this book: Use a running journal, either online or a paper copy; find a good running club or running mentor, either online or in person; and keep your running and training as simple as possible.

The pointers and information included in this book are intended as useful tools to help get rid of the "BUT" phenomenon of starting out: But how far should I run? But am I too old/fat/short/skinny to start running? But don't I need a special watch/shoes/shirt/bra? Our mind can become an incredible mechanism of procrastination. Hopefully this book will help to dismiss these niggling questions and inspire you to get out there and get running.

You can start right away by choosing the right running schedule for you in Chapter 9—Training Schedule for Active Beginners, Training Schedule for Non-Exercisers, Training Schedule for Weight Loss, or Training Schedule for People 50 and Older—and begin running immediately, as long as you feel confident enough to do so.

If you have particular health issues or concerns such as asthma or arthritis, please check with your doctor before beginning.

Something that will be mentioned frequently throughout this book that is not a necessity but can play a very positive role as you begin to run and train: a running journal. It doesn't have to be fancy; simply a notebook where you can record how long you ran, the distance, (which can be as basic as "to the mailbox and back") and other considerations you feel are important. Again, a running journal isn't a necessity, but it is one more psychological tool we can use to help build our confidence and determination.

By keeping note of our runs in a journal we are essentially saying that we are taking ourselves seriously, and that we'll be keeping a record of our goals, setbacks, and successes.

The Mental Health Benefits of Running

As we all know by now, or should know, the body and the mind are inexorably linked, but we will briefly explore here both the mental and physical benefits of running or jogging as if they were separate.

Stress is the number one offender in the cause of health problems today: stress lowers the effectiveness of the immune system and so our bodies become more susceptible to colds and sickness. High blood pressure, heart disease and depression are some of the more lasting effects of chronic stress; while depression, addiction, hair loss, and obesity are also known to be directly linked to stress. What does stress have to do with running?

Epinephrine is a chemical released in our bodies when we get stressed. The synthetic version of this chemical is used to massively increase heart rate and blood pressure for people with severe allergic reactions to bees or certain foods (hence the "epi pen"). Epinephrine is a very powerful stimulant response in our bodies that initially helped humans to survive threatening environments. Epinephrine can give us a quick kick-start to climb a tree faster to get away from a bear, dodge a speeding car, or help someone in need. The production of epinephrine as a basic survival tool is a wonderful thing, and is also produced when we are excited or stressed in a "good" way, which helps us to enjoy roller coasters or water slides that much more.

The problem arises, however, when epinephrine is constantly produced because of chronic stress, instead of only when it's needed. The body and its primal reaction to stress cannot differentiate between an oncoming wildebeest mamma protecting her young, or an upcoming presentation at the office . . . a traffic jam or a rockslide . . . a recital or a true battle. You get the idea.

With the production of epinephrine the body essentially shuts down all non-essential functions to send oxygen to major muscle groups, the heart, and increase body temperature. Thus the immune system, digestion, and sleep cycles are all interrupted and affected by stress and the *unnecessary* production of epinephrine.

When we are chronically, persistently stressed, epinephrine levels eventually lower, while still being created in the body, leaving us feeling exhausted and often depressed, even if we've gotten 'a good night's sleep' or have spent the weekend frolicking. Chronic stress is the result of triggering the primitive "fight or flight" response of our bodies, but we do neither. Day after day our bodies tell us to deal with stressors in some way; yet in modern society, regrettably, we value money, time, and "staying busy" more than we do meditation, rest, and exercise.

Endurance exercises and less stressful training, such as running, help to rid the body of epinephrine while helping us to relax and stop the constant production of epinephrine. Exercise also helps the body to process stress hormones— instead of fighting the "fight or flight" response our bodies naturally have and simply "putting up with it," whatever "it" may be—we are able to release tension, sweat, and metabolize stress in a healthy manner.

Interestingly, many people engage in difficult exercise regimens to combat feelings of exhaustion and depression, which can then also create (and deplete) epinephrine. They may feel great while the intensity of their exercise keeps adrenaline levels up, but are perplexed when, several hours after exercising, their mood elevation plummets once again. Arduous stop/start exercises such as basketball and football, or more "extreme" sports create a great adrenaline rush (the twin of epinephrine), but do not help to assuage stress as a nice long jog or run does.

With running we are not creating externally stressful situations to raise our heart rate. When we run we gradually build and maintain a pace; our bodies and minds aren't worrying about the next shot, pass, or hairpin curve. And so our bodies reap all the benefits of exercise without the jolts of adrenaline and epinephrine created in more "extreme" sports and hobbies.

Not to be mistaken, practically speaking any exercise is good exercise, but just as there is "good" and "bad" stress in our lives, there are times when the body and mind need less epinephrine and adrenaline. Good stress allows us to rise to the occasions of our lives and to better deal with difficult situations. As noted, bad stress arises when we don't have the ability to turn off our stress reactions, resulting in clenched jaws, headaches, and other serious health issues.

Less arduous exercises centered on gradually increasing fitness help to create more serotonin. While epinephrine can be a body's reaction to stress and triggers an intense survival response, serotonin is the chemical our bodies produce to let us know that we're safe, comfortable, and able to relax; to let down our defenses.

Can we control how much serotonin our bodies produce? Can we have some control over our stress levels and mood?

The short answer is yes, we can.

Long- and middle-distance running in particular are sports that create a rise in serotonin levels, which in turn have an effect on the dopamine levels in our bodies, the chemical that produces our rest and sleep patterns.

Because epinephrine and serotonin are so closely linked (both are released during exercise, but only epinephrine in stressful situations) when we run at low-to-moderate intensity levels we not only help our bodies, but we become better able to take advantage of our rest. Our bodies repair themselves more efficiently, and we fall sick less often . . .

We become less stressed and more able to handle our lives effectively.

The ability to deal with stress in our daily lives is

arguably *the* most important part of our day-to-day existence. Stress can affect every part of our life including work, relationships, and overall health. In running, we find a way to keep the body healthy, as well as a positive outlet for stress, and time for contemplation.

Aside from the positive biochemical reaction that consistent exercise creates, the psychological benefits of running are extremely rewarding. Running builds confidence few other sports can because there is no reliance on equipment, events, matches, or other people—running depends entirely on us. Although this may seem daunting to runners just starting out, it soon becomes our greatest asset—every time we step out the door and trot off into the distance, we gain a little mental and physical health, discipline and confidence.

Being able to slip on a comfortable pair of sneakers and ease down a favorite street, park, or trail while building self-confidence offers many people the motivation they need to get off the couch and get running.

Of course running is not the panacea for all of our ills, but it does offer us the chance to escape the daily grind for a short while and focus on the things that really matter in our lives: breathing, maintaining a steady rhythm, thinking about family and friends, enjoying the countryside.

The Physical Health Benefits of Running

Running works more major muscle groups *and* the cardiovascular system harder and more efficiently than many other sports. If you follow a fairly strict regimen such as the Training Schedules in Chapter 9, you can hope to see results in as little as thirty days; more importantly, you should *feel* the benefits of getting outside and exercising almost immediately.

Because running builds lean muscle it helps increase the metabolism (the basic rate at which our bodies burn calories), which in turn burns more calories. Muscle burns more calories than fat, and so we runners get the advantage of strength, stamina, and eventually burning fat calories even when we're not running!

The two largest muscle groups in the body, the thighs and butt, get the primary benefit from brisk walking, jogging, and running; but running is also great for the "core" of the body: abdomen, chest, and upper arms. Combined with warming up, stretching, a few push-ups, pull-ups, and some sit-ups at the beginning or end of a workout, running *is* the original (and best) total-body workout.

It should be noted that as we build lean muscle and replace the fat in our body with muscle, especially in our thighs and posteriors, we may actually notice we've gained a few pounds. Along with a few other factors such as our bodies holding onto water to help recovering muscles and increased appetite, this is not uncommon. Not to worry. Muscle is dense and vascular, and as we build it, it tips the scales, even if it is just a small quantity. Compared to fat, which takes up a lot of space per pound, muscle does not, and it consumes a lot more energy. Therefore, progress cannot be measured by the total mass of the body. A reliable measure is the fat to muscle ratio, which is improving. Body composition will show an increase in lean body mass, and a decrease in fat mass as your body leans out. Base your progress, then, not on the scale but on the measuring tape, mental benefits, and the act that you've gone from being able to run for only 20 seconds, for example, to 20 minutes!

Women in particular have a higher body fat percentage and less testosterone than men, and despite what weight-loss reality shows depict, the playing field isn't level for men and women in the beginning. However, as our training progresses and the intensity of our workouts increases we discover that the overall health and feeling of well-being is secondary to weight loss. If we are dedicated and watch our nutrition, the weight will take care of itself.

Aside from body image though, there is virtually nothing in our physical bodies that running doesn't affect in a positive way. When our cardiovascular system improves, so does our blood pressure because of the workout our arteries get. The healthier our arteries are, the less prone we are to heart problems, particularly heart disease, which is currently the number one cause of death in the United States and is called a "global epidemic" by the World Health Organization.

Jogging and brisk walking are also frequently used to treat diabetes, depression, and addiction. By building stronger bones and muscle tissue we are able to slow down the signs and symptoms of aging and maintain our endurance, which includes sex drive. Yes, rather than expensive pills with strange side effects, running can even make us happier in the sack.

The most important benefit to a good exercise regimen, though, seems to be its part in helping to reduce cancer. In one study done in Finland, it was found that Finnish men who regularly exercised at a fairly intense level, including running, had *a 50% less chance of developing prostate cancer than those who didn't.* [1]

Although the research is still somewhat controversial, it would seem that 30 minutes of increased heart-rate exercise four to five times a week dramatically reduces the potential of cancer. This includes breast, lung, pancreatic, and ovarian cancer. Exercise, in particular running, also seems to be particularly effective in reducing the chances of getting colon cancer.

As mentioned, there really is no way to separate our minds and bodies. The healthy psychological changes produced from exercise and running have a positive effect on our bodies, which then makes us stronger and more resistant to sickness and disease. Because we are all so different in mind, body, and temperament, research will probably never wholly agree on the specific benefits of jogging and running. But common sense and a little personal experience will soon tell us what we intuitively already know: a little running can take us a long way, in mind *and* body.

Chapter 1: Getting Ready to Run

This chapter will cover a lot of information for beginner runners, with a detailed breakdown of proper running form and mechanics. If you have a specific question, skip to the subtopic of your choice for a quick answer. And if you feel confident you're ready to start running, by all means skip to the Training Schedule for Active Beginner Runners, or one of the other Running Schedules in Chapter 9, and start running! As you begin to run, you may have specific questions that will be answered in these chapters, and there's no substitute for the real thing to get those questions going.

One of the first things we can do to help ourselves prepare is to start a running journal. This journal can be as general as or as specific as you would like. Some runners record times and distances diligently, while others use a running journal as more of a diary to record fears, triumphs, challenges, and successes.

Below is a very general example of some topics you can include in a running log and how they would look in a spreadsheet:

Date	Time Ran	Distance or Landmark	Shoe Milage	Pre-Run Meal	Post-Run Meal	Notes	Goal(s) and Progress
12/1	43:15	Third mailbox and back	2nd month @150 miles	Celery w/peanut butter	Pasta w/alfredo sauce	Stiff headwind, but felt great!	Closing in on that 40 min. mark

There are also many online running logs, both for free and for purchase, along with calorie calculators and other useful tools for runners. A running log is invaluable in tracking your route from tentative beginner to accomplished runner!

A Note on Running Form and Footwear

Although footwear will be covered in the next chapter, keep in mind that these two topics are inexorably linked—a runner may have the best running form in the world, but if she is wearing old basketball sneakers, she's bound to get shin splints and knee problems.

The opposite is true as well—a $150 pair of running shoes won't do much good for someone with terrible running form.

The Mechanics of Form

Let's start with running form, as good form will greatly help increase your comfort and efficiency on initial runs. The basic mantra for running is, "Run comfortably, but run disciplined." This may sound contradictory, but it reminds us to keep our shoulders, chest, and neck loose while maintaining good posture; to keep our shoulders and elbows moving in a forward direction (not side-to-side) while keeping all of our movements fluid. We should have a slight *whole body* forward lean, being careful not to bend at the waist.

Running form is broken down into two parts: the stance phase and the swing phase. Stance phase occurs when the foot comes in contact with the ground, while swing phase is when the foot is in the air. Running differs from walking in that at some point in the running cycle, both feet are in the air simultaneously, no matter how slow we are moving!

With walking, however, one foot is always in contact with the ground. The energy taken to essentially jump from one foot to another is one of the reasons that running is more physically demanding than walking. With every footfall, the force of nearly three times your body weight is transmitted throughout your lower leg. (This is yet another one of the many reasons to have good running form!)

Foot Strike

How should your feet fall when you run? The proper positioning of the foot, "foot strike," is important for preventing injury and reducing stress on the joints. The following describes the **Midfoot strike**, which is widely used by runners at all levels.

Ideally, your foot should strike the ground on the midfoot, and not crash land on your heel. To find your midfoot, stand with both feet flat on the floor. Shift your weight forward to lift your heels ¼ inch off the ground. We're not quite on our toes, and definitely not on our heels. On the next page, we describe how to progress to a midfoot strike. A simple way of finding the midfoot is by skipping rope rapidly with very shallow jumps. The point of contact is at the front edge of the arch in the foot, sometimes called the "ball of your feet", which keeps contact with the ground brief and effective.

Many runners have a natural heel strike that that they tend towards which works fine; only occasionally do we need to adjust our natural stride because our heels may be striking first, causing pain or shin splints in the lower leg.

Mid-stance: Once your foot has landed on the ground, your arch, Achilles tendon, and calf absorb the pressure of your landing. The foot rolls inwards as your arch flattens along the ground, a movement called pronation.

Everyone needs a certain amount of pronation to allow your body to absorb impact and to bring it into an efficient running position. It is when someone over or under pronates that we begin to have problems with injuries and soreness, which will be discussed later.

Toe-off: As your midfoot absorbs ground pressure during mid-stance, your toes flatten out and it is your big toe that leaves the ground last as the body moves forward. It is sometimes thought that the large joint in your big toe is the most important joint in your body for proper and efficient running form; the toe flexes at almost 70° in preparation of pushing off for the next stride.

Swing phase: (while the foot is in the air): In this phase of our stride the legs actually swing in toward the middle of the body and then out again slightly as the leg moves through the air. We don't feel this as we run because it is so natural, but if our hips are sore after the first few initial runs, it is probably due to this rotation of the leg as we are in the air. The powerful hip muscles and hip flexors do a lot of the work when we run.

Of course the upper body is very important as well. The right arm is connected to the left leg and the left arm is connected to your right leg, both on a neurological and anatomical level. Although it's been guessed at for years, new studies show definitively that tissue connections (fascia) cross at the midsection of the body in both the front and the back of the body, connecting the opposing limbs.[2] Our overall strength and balance are crucial for good running form; we not only build leg strength and endurance by running, but we also work out the upper body and abdomen the more we run. Because running requires so much inter-body coordination it will help us to seek out and destroy the weak links of our body.

Does all of this information about anatomy and body mechanics really matter for us as beginner runners? You bet. A huge benefit to running is the knowledge and awareness of our bodies as we run. The more we know about ourselves, the more we can marvel at the incredible interconnectedness of all our body parts (from jaw to big toe) that help to keep us in fluid motion. Also, by knowing that our right arm is connected to our left leg, for example, we are better able to determine our weaknesses and possible reasons for lingering pains or injuries.

Midfoot Strike Learning Progression:

Perform 5 to 10 rhythmic repetitions of each: Start by hopping on both feet (imagine skipping rope). Next, alternate from your left to right foot. Now lift your heels up. Finally, allow yourself to move forward with each hop. Gradually increase speed when you are comfortable. You can use this as a part of your warm up as well.

3 Common Questions About Running Mechanics

Q: Is heel strike a bad thing?

A: For some, heel strike is a more natural way of running. Heel striking leads to problems when the knee isn't flexed enough, causing the shock of impact not to be absorbed. Many argue in favor of heel striking because it works for them. Knee and hip pain often arise from people who heel strike so it has been generally considered a less safe way to run.

Q: What about foot pronation? Isn't it a "bad" thing? How will I know if I am over or under pronating?

A: Foot pronation is necessary for walking and running and we do it hundreds, maybe even thousands of times a day. The muscles in our legs develop around the stride we use for walking and running, so as long as we're training gradually there shouldn't be problems, even if we're "pigeon-toed" or have high or low arches. You will have to start looking at pronation issues if the inside or outside of your feet are continually sore or achy, or if you persistently develop shin splints and/or knee problems. You'll also be able to tell if you are over or under pronating from the wear and tear on the soles of your shoes.

Q: What if I have terrible running form, but am comfortable in the way that I run?

A: If you are training for long-distance runs such as a marathon, this could be a problem. If you are running for fun and fitness, however, then run in the way that feels most natural to you, while *gradually* working to improve your form and mechanics. Remember that heel or forefoot striking is not necessarily bad, or hazardous, but rather it is not *ideal*.

Common Mistakes and Tips for Improving Form Arms and Hands

One of the most common mistakes that beginner runners make is pumping their elbows from side to side as if elbowing folks out of the way to get to the front of a line.

Our hand movements are crucial in that they not only control the motions of our shoulders, but also the hips. If our hands and lower arms aren't swinging up in a natural way, then the shoulders are shrugging side to side, which in turn rotates the lower body and hips in a completely inefficient and awkward manner. Some runners term this the "runway jog," because it looks as if the runner is tipsily moving down a runway in high heels!

Arms Tip #1

It may be a bit uncomfortable at first, but always try to imagine a string tied from the little finger of each hand to the little toe of each foot. Although our hands and feet should alternate (right hand up with left knee up/left hand up with right knee up) the "string trick" is a helpful mental reminder to keep everything moving in line.

Arms Tip #2

Another little trick we may use is the pistol approach. This is employed more often with sprinters, but is also useful in short and middle distance running. The idea is to imagine your hands as pistols—while keeping your palms slightly open, the index finger loosely points straight ahead. As each hand swings up, you are "shooting" at a target located directly in front of you, approximately thirty yards distant at waist level.

This accomplishes keeping our eyes up, our hands and feet moving straight forward, and our posture erect. Even when shooting bad guys in the distance, our hands should always be loose, fluid, and not cross above the chest. Our arms are important in maintaining pace, but excessive arm motion leads to wasted energy.

Clenched fists translate up the arm muscles to tight shoulders, which causes our running to be wooden, tightens the chest, and creates labored breathing.

Hands Tip #1

Yet one more little device is to make a teardrop shape from the forefinger and thumb, with the rest of the fingers in line with the index finger. "Don't squish the bug," between the thumb and forefinger, is a common piece of advice.

This is simply another way to keep the shoulders, arms and hands from tensing up when fatigue sets in or we are pushing ourselves particularly hard. As runs become longer, "shaking out" our arms to loosen them up and relax them as we run may become common.

More accomplished runners may seem to not be moving their arms at all. These long-distance runners are employing an economy of movement that appears natural, but is actually the result of a lot of training and discipline.

Good runners appear as if they have been to finishing school and a couple of books could be placed on top of their head and the books would stay there throughout a marathon—their postures and the elimination of any wasted movement of the upper body help them to appear as if they are gliding above the ground instead of running a grueling race. If this is confusing, watch different clips of professional runners, paying especially close attention to the heads, arms, and shoulders. You will find that although professional runners often have vastly different *styles* from one another, their basic *form* is the same.

The longer a person runs, the more running comes to feel natural, and at a certain stage we hope to feel our arms relaxing, our legs moving effortlessly beneath us, our upper bodies moving so efficiently that it *looks* as if hardly any effort is involved at all.

Feet

Keeping all of this in mind, hopefully, we now concentrate on the feet. The center of the foot should usually be hitting first (not to be mistaken for landing flat-footed), rolling to the ball of the foot, before pushing off for the next stride. "Smooth" is the key word with our feet.

Disclaimer

Since all of our fitness levels, legs, and feet are different, beware of anyone who prescribes a very specific way for foot strike. Ultra runners (professional athletes) will be running at the front end of their feet, using mostly the ball and toes of the foot, some runners will land in the middle of the foot, while some may run for years and still have a slight heel strike. This doesn't negate all good running form advice; it just reminds us to keep it simple and comfortable. What keeps you enjoying running and injury-free is always the best running method for you!

Feet Tip #1

If it feels like your feet are jolting the entire leg every time they hit the ground, you are probably heel striking and the heel is acting as a brake. Try to shorten your stride a little; you can still maintain a good pace even with a shorter stride by quickening the cadence, or rhythm, of your stride.

This should keep you from locking your knee as you stride out. Picture a bicycle rider and the motion used for pedaling a bike: this cyclical rhythm and keeping the feet below the body's center of gravity gives us a good idea about how the motion of our feet should look.

Feet Tip #2

Run across the lawn barefoot. We should all do this at some point because it's just plain fun, but in this case the exercise gives us a good idea of how our "natural" stride and foot strike feels without shoes.

We'll find that as we run barefoot we place our feet more carefully on the ground and run more toward the front of the foot than in shoes. No doubt we will run differently in shoes, there's no getting around that fact. You may want to consider minimalist shoes, especially if you find this form more comfortable on your joints! However we can be aware if we are using our shoes as a crutch for bad running form, such as being lazy with our feet as we fatigue, and allowing our feet to flop instead of placing our feet one in front of the other.

Feet Tip #3

Take a few minutes at the beginning of a run and try to emulate a cross-country skier. Practice gliding and pushing across the ground, even if it looks and feels a little silly. Cross-country skiers move their feet parallel to each other and get a good deal of spring from the arches of their feet and toes, despite their feet never leaving the ground. Taking a few minutes to glide and kick as a skier would gives us a good idea of smooth arm motion and foot placement. (If you feel uncomfortable doing this in public, practice "gliding" around the house in socks.)

Feet Tip #4

If it sounds as if someone were clapping their hands every time you run, practicing "quiet" running is another great exercise. Some runners simply haven't grown into their feet, while others seem to be angry with their feet, the ground, or both.

Quiet running doesn't mean running entirely on your toes or running slower, but focusing on *placing* your feet on the ground as you run, as mentioned above. The difference between "muscling" the feet and placing the feet is the same difference between *swinging* a baseball bat to meet the ball, for example, and pushing a bat toward a ball.

It may feel strange at first, but exaggerate the motions of quiet running into the first few minutes of every run until it becomes a more natural part of your running style. "Slappy" feet and clunky heels will cause you to run slower and less distance, but more importantly this bad form is hard on the fragile bones of your feet, lower legs and knees.

Overall-Form Improvement

The techniques and tips written here are all things you can work on and improve by yourself. As you get more serious, though, it is always a good idea to have someone look at your running style to give you pointers on how to improve.

Overall-Form Tip #1

A treadmill is one way to work on your form in a 'closed' environment, particularly one with the large mirror in which you can watch yourself as you run.

Overall-Form Tip #2

Another way to improve your overall running technique is to practice running in water. At your local pool or on a hot summer day in a nearby pond, immerse yourself about waist deep in the water, fix your eyes at a set point and begin moving towards it. Because water is less forgiving than air, as you fatigue, if you're still paying attention, you'll notice yourself veering to the left or right, dropping or clenching the hands, or leaning too far forward to try and muscle your way through the water. This slow-motion exercise is a great way to become conscious of how our body parts work together (or don't) to create a fluid running form.

Breathing

Finally, we come to breathing. The key phrase here is *control your breathing; don't let your breathing control you.* This is much easier said than done, but if you employ the techniques of good form mentioned above, good breathing *will* become second nature.

Establish a good, steady pace, perhaps even counting out the rhythm of your feet in your mind: one, two, three, four, . . . and then, without too much effort on your part or forcibly changing your breathing suddenly, begin to exhale at 1,2,3 and inhale at 4; still at a rate that is comfortable for you *at the pace you're running.* Do not try and match your breathing with a pace in which we would *like* to run—we cannot outrun our breath, so to speak. Attempting to run faster than our lung capacity often happens to novice runners and creates a very uneven and panicky run, at best.

Find your best breathing rate and adjust your movements to that rate. If you follow the Running Schedules diligently, you'll find that when you become winded you will eventually be able to control and slow your breathing without having to slow your pace. Initially, though, simply focus on keeping your upper body loose, and breathing *through* your diaphragm, mentally from the very bottom of your stomach.

Breathing Tip #1

Try not to focus too much on breathing at any given time—come back to your breathing intermittently during a run, always remembering that you are in control of your breathing. If you feel that you are breathing too hard, slow down; if you are breathing *too* comfortably, perhaps this means it's time to gradually elevate your pace.

Breathing Tip #2

Breathing while running should always be primarily through the mouth, but both your mouth and your nose will be utilized to supply the lungs with oxygen.

That being said, nose breathing has a long and interesting history, with certain Native American runners recorded as running for miles with a mouthful of water to maintain nose breathing. Or, more commonly, a small pebble would be placed in the mouth to help keep the mouth from getting too dry. The main advantage of being able to breathe through the nose while running is that the nose acts as a humidifier for the lungs, enabling a runner to cover longer distances without becoming parched.

Breathing Tip #3

Imagine your lungs as balloons; when you inhale the balloons are being filled, and when you exhale the balloons are being released. Singers employ this method of breathing, which allows for a steadier intake and release of air, versus an all-in, all-out breathing that causes panting and hyperventilation.

Running form seems to be a lot to remember initially, but our bodies know what to do. Much of what is discussed here will come naturally. There have been many long-distance runners who have been wonderfully successful with absolutely awful form; for the majority of us, though, the best way to improve our strength, endurance, and speed is to gradually improve our form. Every runner's form will be slightly different, but all should have in common a form that is comfortable and cohesive—all parts working together to smoothly move straight forward. Consistently working on our running form will help us to train smarter and more efficiently, which, in the end, will pay larger dividends than simply working out harder.

Proper Running Form Summary

- Run comfortably, yet disciplined.

- We want to be balanced in all our movements, neither striding too far with the legs nor reaching too far with the arms.

- Keep head up and eyes focused in the middle distance to retain posture and breathing.

- Keep hands loose and arms relaxed, always moving in a straight forward direction, not side to side.

- Run as "quietly" and as smoothly as you can, rolling your feet beneath you as you run.

- Be mindful that proper foot strike prevents injury and joint stress.

- Aim to keep a breathing rhythm that matches the rhythm and pace of your feet.

- Breathe from the bottom of the diaphragm to prevent panting.

- Proper form can help to make running more enjoyable, less painful, and improve running performance.

Chapter 2: Footwear and Common Foot Problems

We always want to be nice to our feet, but particularly when starting a running regimen. Running shoe discussions can start a fistfight among an otherwise pacifistic and genteel group of people—some runners will stick with the same brand of shoes for years, others will grab a pair of used shoes every chance they get from the Salvation Army because they wear out shoes so fast. Taken altogether it can be a touchy issue. We will try to stay generic here, hopefully without causing undue offense!

Footwear Tip #1

One of the best things we can do for ourselves when we initially start training is to find a shoe store that specializes in running shoes and have them size our feet. We may be surprised to find the size 7 we thought we were wearing all of these years has turned into a 71/2, or vice-versa. Often our feet flatten and enlarge as we grow older, and it's a good idea to get a "foot check-up" every year or so. Occasionally, too, there are people whose feet might be as much as a half-size larger than the other foot. Everyone's foot size varies slightly, but for some it's more dramatic and they should order custom-sized shoes.

Another advantage to going to a shoe store where you'll receive personal attention is that they can offer the best brand of shoe for your foot type. Finding the right shoes for high arches, for example, is as important as finding the right shoe for "flat" feet, or feet with small arches. Certain brands are known for different qualities, and a well-informed salesperson can help point you in the right direction.

Much like finding a good car mechanic, or a good family

dentist, don't be afraid to search out and find a shoe store and staff who will help you find the right shoe for the amount of training you will be doing and the unique qualities of your feet.

A good way to tell if a shoe store is right for you is to ask if you can take a pair of shoes for a quick test run/walk. A good shoe shop, particularly those geared specifically toward runners, will not only allow you to walk or jog around, but will encourage this to ensure a good buy. If a shoe store won't allow you to stroll or jog around the block, then it's not a store you want to give money to.

Yet another aspect of a good running shoe store is their willingness to take back shoes that don't fit comfortably; there should be no hesitation on the part of the store to take back shoes that genuinely don't work for you.

Footwear Tip #2

It's said that many fishing lures are designed more to catch the eye of the fisherman instead of the fish; this also seems to be true of shoes. No matter how tempting, do not choose a shoe because of how it looks, the advertising surrounding it, or simply because it's the highest priced. These can all be factors, of course, but the first consideration should always be the fit and support of the shoe.

For most novice runners (and for many serious runners, although they won't admit it) a basic pair of running shoes will work fine. Also, with cheaper "off-brand" shoes, or last year's models of name-brand shoes, there isn't as much temptation to stick with an uncomfortable shoe because of its cost. We are more apt to recycle a pair of running shoes and get a new pair when they've cost us $30 dollars versus

$130 dollars.

Footwear Tip #3

Finding a shoe that fits comfortably, protects the instep (or arch) of your foot, and cushions the heel are the most important factors when selecting a shoe. Other factors when fitting a shoe include:

- You should be able to wiggle your toes in the *toe box*, or tip of the shoe.

- Your foot should feel snug in the heel, and there should be no rubbing or slipping when your foot stretches for the next stride. Your heel or Achilles tendon should not feel pinched in any way.

- You should have reasonable flexibility in the forefoot/toe area. (Try flexing the shoe slightly up toward the rear of the shoe with your hand. The shoe should bend easily just behind where the ball of the foot would be.) For trail running, this midsole should be stiffer, providing a more stable base.

- The shoe should fit snugly across the top of the foot to prevent slipping, but should never be so snug as to cut off circulation. In addition, the tongue of the shoe should be padded enough to keep the shoe laces from irritating, or cutting into, the top of your foot.

- Shoes or laces that are too tight are often the cause of numb toes.

Footwear Tip #4

Remember to recycle your old running shoes. There are many different local and national organizations that take old shoes; some are shipped to other countries for people in need of shoes and shoe materials. Others, like Nike, will take your shoes and recycle them to create different surfaces for tracks, playgrounds, etc. Old shoes also make for a great planter for your small plants!

Nowadays the main difference between different models of shoes is not the comfort, as it once was. The major difference now between shoes seems to be durability. As a general rule, a bit more money paid for a pair of shoes means they will last longer, although this is, of course, not always the case.

How long should a good pair of shoes last? This depends on how often and how far you run, but six months is a good rule of thumb. You should be able to get 300-400 miles out of a pair of shoes depending on your size, the distance and duration of your runs, and whether or not you are running on concrete or asphalt. It's a good idea to buy a new pair of shoes around the mid-life point of the old shoes to have as a comparison model in how they both look and feel. Use the newer pair of shoes to gauge when the midsole of the older pair is wearing out and is no longer supporting your foot properly.

As your shoes become worn down, study the soles to find out where you are putting the most wear: you should see a fairly even wear pattern, with the ball of the foot and the heel showing the most use. Another good reason to have and use two pairs of shoes: as our shoes wear down to our own peculiar foot patterns it may tend to accentuate pronation issues by having too much wear on one side, front or back. By keeping our shoes "fresh" and balanced, it helps to keep our feet balanced too.

Footwear Tip #5

General care tips to help your shoes last longer:

- Wipe off the shoes with a slightly damp cloth after running in dusty, wet, or muddy conditions.

- Ensure the shoes have dried from the previous run.

- Have two pairs of shoes and alternate them to allow time to dry and decompress. Also, alternating shoes helps to ward off "foot funk" which will make you more popular with your housemates.

- Hand wash shoes and set them out to dry instead of using washing and drying machines.

- Only wear your running shoes to run/exercise; they might be the most comfortable shoes you have, but your running shoes should be used exclusively for running. (Having said that, wearing a new pair of shoes around the house for a day or two will help to break them in.)

Footwear Tip #6

Your running journal is a great place to jot down when and where you bought your shoes, cost, how much use you got out of the pair of shoes, how well they held up, and some general notes about how the shoes worked for you. This will allow you to remember your preferences as you continue your running career. Remember to jot down wear areas on the soles and "hot spots," or spots where your shoes caused you pain. By writing these things down you will be able to look back and see if there are recurring problems and if these problems are caused by the shoes, your running form, or both.

Insoles have advanced enough in recent years that many runners will buy a basic, fairly cheap pair of running shoes and replace the insoles with a set of insoles of their own choosing. Insoles can run anywhere from $10-$20 to ridiculous. There are insoles to help support high arches, or to add support for low arches, otherwise known as "flat" feet, or any combination in between. Essentially, there are insoles made to help with whatever foot problems you may have, or whatever cushioning or support your shoes lack, so don't give up on your shoes before trying out a set of insoles.

If your feet are being very difficult, there are even manufacturers that offer insoles that you heat in the oven and microwave, and then place your feet onto, effectively molding the insole to the shape of your feet.

Common Foot Problems and Easy Solutions

Certain foot problems will be dealt with in Chapter 7, but suffice to say that when you buy your new sneakers you should probably buy some "Moleskin" along with them. (Not to be confused with the wonderful writing notebooks by Moleskine.)

Moleskin has tough interwoven sheered cotton on one side, while the other has an adhesive that sticks to the skin. Properly cut and placed, Moleskin is a life saver when it comes to blisters and corns. Some diehard runners will place a piece of duct tape over a "hot" spot (a spot where rubbing has occurred, but a blister has not yet formed), but this should be done as an absolute last resort. The slick side of the tape does ease friction and it's much thinner than Moleskin, but taking the duct tape off of an already-tender spot can be a little uncomfortable, to say the least!

One way to ward off blisters before they start is a good pair of liner socks. Most runners balk at wearing two pairs of socks while running because of the bulk; but a very thin, breathable pair of sock liners can help to ease friction, particularly in the Achilles and heel areas where most shoes are prone to rub. If you are changing your routine (doing more hills, or more flat ground) or are just beginning your workouts with new shoes, it never hurts to wear a pair of liners along with a pair of regular socks.

Short Introduction to Pronation

If you have high arches in your feet you *may* tend to under-pronate. Don't worry, this is not a dirty word or a disease, but simply the way your foot turns as it rolls towards the toe. As the name suggests, if you tend to under-pronate, you *may* not rotate your foot as much to the inside as is desirable, creating strain on the outside of your foot. If your little toes and the outside of your foot are sore after running, with sore muscles surrounding the upper shin, this *may* mean you need to find footwear or insoles to help correct this problem. Same thing applies if the ball of your feet and big toe are chronically sore, which would be over-pronating to the inside of the foot. (The emphasis on *may* comes from this being a very individual and complicated topic with many variables.)

Despite what many shoe and insole companies try to tell and sell us, under- and over-pronation are generally caused by the movements in our hips. This goes back again to running form, and the motion of our arms and the core muscles of our stomach and chest, which in a large degree control the motion of our hips.

The only time we beginner runners truly need to worry about pronation is if we are experiencing a lot of discomfort in our toes from over- or under-pronation; or have recurring shin splint problems (a dull ache or pain, usually in the front of the leg caused by lack of arch support or muscle overuse).

If this is the case, first try a few runs while thinking about the movement of your arms and upper body in connection with your hips. Next, get off of the pavement if at all possible and run on a track, path, or anything more forgiving than asphalt. If these methods fail, then it may be time to look at more substantial solutions such as custom-made insoles or shoes.

If you are unsure what type of arch you have, walk with wet feet across a tile or wooden floor—the imprints left on the surface should tell you what type of arch your feet have. If you leave a slender quarter-moon imprint, then you have higher arches; if almost the entire bottom of your foot shows in your imprint then your feet have lower arches.

Whether or not we should be concerned with our high or low arches or pronation issues is yet another reason to be on good terms with the staff at your local shoe store. They should be able to tell you without too much difficulty what brand of shoes help with pronation and arch problems, and possibly even give you a quick test on a treadmill to tell whether or not it could be a problem for you as a runner.

Keep It Simple

Remember as a novice runner you will be discovering the finer points of form and footwear slowly—along with gradually building endurance, muscles, and your cardio system. As with most things in life, these two topics—

footwear and form—can be greatly overthought. Keep it simple, and try to be proactive and act before problems become persistent.

Buy basic shoes until you know exactly what you need and want out of a shoe. Keep in mind what your body, and especially your feet, are telling you about your running. This includes distance, intensity, environment, and form—adjust accordingly. Running is enjoyable as a sport or a hobby, and though some discomfort is inevitable, we should never try to "tough it out" or push ourselves too hard too soon.

The Running Schedules, again, included in Chapter 9 are a great way to take the guesswork out of trying to determine our initial workouts.

Footwear Summary

- Buy the best shoes you can afford, but remember that a more expensive shoe does not always mean a higher quality shoe.

- Find a good shoe store with a knowledgeable, helpful staff, even if it means paying a little bit extra for a pair of shoes.

- Shoes should be comfortably snug with particular attention to cushioning the heel and supporting the arch.

- A decent mid-level shoe can be "upgraded" with a good set of insoles.

- Try to be proactive with your feet—protect hot spots with Moleskin or other adhesives before blisters have a chance to form.

- Staff at a good shoe store can tell you if you over- or under-pronate, and will help you find the best type of shoe for your needs.

Chapter 3: Warming Up, Cooling Down, and Target Heart Rates

Warming Up and Stretching

As with many other aspects of running, there is a lot dissension on the topic of stretching and its effectiveness in preventing injury and soreness. Running in all of its different facets will always be a solo sport; individual runners will have to decide for themselves what types of stretches they do, and when stretching will work best for them.

For now, we'll employ some common sense and experience to set out general guidelines for stretching before and after a run.

How to Warm Up Before a Run

Generally speaking, "cold," or static stretching does little for our muscles. Starting out at a brisk walk, and then jogging a short distance to elevate the heart rate and send oxygen and blood to the muscles is much more effective in preparing the body to run.

Despite traditional wisdom, as runners we are not actually seeking to "stretch" anything; what we want to do is to *warm up* to increase oxygen and blood flow, which in turns *loosens up* our muscles, joints, and tendons in anticipation of the upcoming run.

An example of how to do this would be to briskly walk/jog for several minutes until the heart rate is elevated and a light sweat starts. Then, starting at the neck and head, roll your head around until your neck feels relaxed. Do *not* roll your head 360 degrees around – this is unsafe for your spine. Instead roll from one side, to the middle, to the other side and then back again the same way.

Next, move to the chest and shoulders, doing windmills, shrugging your shoulders, or simply shaking out your arms until the upper body feels loose.

The trunk should be similar, using rolling movements as if whirling a hula-hoop to loosen up tight or cold joints and muscles, while avoiding "static" stretching whereupon you simply stretch to reach your toes or stretch from a sitting position for thirty seconds.

If the backs of your legs and calves feel tight, place your palms against a wall or tree, while keeping your back foot fully on the ground. The front foot should also be flat against the ground, and you should feel the stretch in the back of your leg in the front foot, while the calf and Achilles tendon feel the stretch in the rear foot.

Because we still don't want to be static while stretching, be sure to look slowly side to side as you stretch as if you're peering over your shoulder—you should be able to actually feel this in your legs, which will give you an idea of how our body parts are so incredibly interconnected, and why posture and eye target are vastly important in running.

You can also begin your breathing during this time, filling your lungs deeply through the nose, and exhaling through your mouth, saturating your body with oxygen and getting a sense of the rhythm you would like to maintain for your run. (Remember, though, that as you begin running your nose won't be efficient in keeping the body supplied with enough oxygen.)

This method of stretching may seem a little odd at first—and look a little strange as you are rolling, hopping and jiggling limbs about—but as we make it part of our routine it will become second nature.

3 Post-Run Stretches

After we have slowed to a walk and given our muscles and joints a good loosening, similar to the warm up, we can gently stretch our muscles and tendons in the more traditional manner. Three good post-run stretches are:

- The hurdler stretch: Sit on the ground placing one leg straight out in front of you, while the other leg is tucked inside, heel to groin. Slowly reach toward the right foot with the right hand, and vice-versa, moving down the shin with your hand, with your chin tucked to your chest to promote spine expansion. The goal of this stretch is *not* to touch your toes and bend them toward you (although that's great if you can do it), but to loosen and elongate the back and neck muscles *while* stretching the back of the leg.

- The butterfly squat: Squat on the toes and place the hands between your legs on the ground. Using the elbows, slowly spread your knees apart to help stretch the groin, while simultaneously rolling your neck. Then, keeping your hands, or at least fingertips, on the ground, slowly straighten the legs. This stretch, when done correctly, stretches the lower back, upper spine, and the backs of the legs. We should be very conscious of the inter-connectedness of our hamstrings, glutes and quadriceps (thighs) during this stretch.

- The downward/upward dog: This stretch is taken from yoga and helps to get us focused back on our "core," the lower body and abdomen. Start in a push-up position on hands and toes (or knees and hands if that's more comfortable for you), and slowly lower your hips (really the lower back) while at the same time raising your head as if looking at the sky. Then lower your head and raise your back to form an inverted "V." Repeat this process several times over.

What If I Experience Muscle Tightening?

If you feel muscles tightening while you run, particularly the large, powerful muscles in the quadriceps, glutes, hamstrings, or Achilles (the large tendon running from the heel through the bottom of the calf), don't hesitate to stop and "talk" to that muscle group. Give it attention by kneading, stretching, or loosening it however feels best, before continuing your run.

Or, you may decide to give that muscle group a break for a few days and go home to ice/heat the area. Alternating heat and ice promotes healing by helping to take the swelling out of inflamed muscles or tendons with ice, while heat helps to increase blood flow to move acid out and bring blood in. The cold/hot regimen essentially "pumps" the small blood vessels by opening and closing them to decrease swelling and inflammation. Always use a cloth or buffer between your skin and ice or an ice pack, and use warm water or a hot water bottle for heat. The heat should not be scalding, in whatever form it takes. Moderate heat is sufficient to open the arteries and promote blood flow.

Because a torn or stretched hamstring, for example, is painful and takes a lot of recovery time, it is *always* best to err on the side of caution. Interrupting the rhythm of a run is an inconvenience, but not as much as missing six weeks or six months of training. (More will be covered on pulled and strained muscles and how to treat them in Chapter 7.)

Warming Up and Stretching Summary

- Try to stay away from static stretches in favor of dynamic stretching and warming up.

- All of the body is interconnected, and so a full-body warm up is always best.

- There is no running rule that says we can't stop mid-run to massage, stretch, and roll tight or sore muscles!

- It's wise to always push ourselves to the utmost of our ability, but never to the point of injury.

- Post-run stretching can be slower and more static.

Cooling Down and Muscle Soreness

This stage of your workout is vastly important, and whenever humanly possible, should not be skipped or skimped on.

Particularly when we are first building lean muscle and getting used to a running regimen, the burning we feel in our muscles when exercising is lactic acid. Lactic acid acts as a super fuel to our muscles, but the burning we feel mid-to-late workout is also a warning sign to let our bodies know muscles aren't receiving enough oxygen. Researchers disagree on whether or not lactic acid buildup is a negative byproduct of intense exercise, but we can be fairly sure that after a good run we need to take about 1/5 of our workout time to gently wind down and get all of the systems in our body stabilized. Lactic acid is the cause of burning muscles while exercising, but it is not necessarily the cause of sore muscles and tissue the next day, although it is often blamed. Exercising actually creates small tears in muscles, which then repair and build new tissue to create new muscle. This is the pain and soreness we feel after exercise. [3]

The cool-down period after a run is vital in helping to ease and prevent soreness. One of the most natural poses a runner will assume after a difficult run is the hands-on-the-knees-head-down pose; while the all-out flop-on-the-back is another. If we think about what this does to our diaphragm, all the muscles and organs in our bodies working at a maximum rate and then "shutting down" in this manner, it should be fairly obvious why this is one of the few "nevers" in running. As enticing as this pose may be after a hard run, keeping your posture and breathing up and open, with hands up or behind your head, is a much more courteous way to thank your body after a run. Try, no matter how tired you feel, to keep moving to promote circulation and gradual stabilization of your breathing and heart rate.

Always try to gradually reduce your exercise until the blood pumping to your extremities can be sent back to the heart and brain. If you've ever seen a runner stop suddenly, and then faint or pass out, the reason was most likely that so much of their blood was pooled in the legs that the sudden stop didn't allow for the heart to push blood to the brain fast enough to prevent them from losing consciousness. This is an extreme example, of course, but gives an idea of how hard our heart is working and how much blood is pumping when we exercise.

Just like warming and loosening up before a run, a steady, easily maintained elevated heart rate helps to spread the oxygen and nutrients needed to repair muscles after a run. Breathing and stretching after a run is almost as important as the run itself and will help us immensely with feeling better mentally and physically post-run.

There is no magic bullet or sports drink that will help immediately repair muscle tissue. Certain drinks, vitamins, and foods *may* help to speed up the recovery process, but we will be better off spending the extra minutes loosening up and stretching after a run instead of guzzling pickle juice, or picking up the next new expensive derivative of chocolate milk.

In determining what to eat or drink post-run, we follow the same rule as in all of running: keep it simple. Our bodies use carbohydrates to produce the different sugars our muscles need to work well. Eat good, "clean" carbs (whole grain rice, oatmeal, pasta, etc.) and protein while training (this will be covered more in-depth in Chapter 6). Drink about 4-6 ounces of water for every 15-20 minutes of exercise, including warm up and cool down periods.

Cool down and Soreness Tip #1

Sipping tepid (lukewarm) water before or after a run as a way to help prevent sore muscles and side aches ("stitches") is a myth. Cold water tastes better, and helps to cool the body's core temperature after a hot run. In various studies, water doesn't have as much of an effect on side pains or stitches as much as the pre-run warm up and proper breathing.

Some runners have advocated carbonated beverages such as Coke or seltzer water as an after-workout drink because the carbonation supposedly hydrates the body faster, but the amount of sugars and empty calories don't compensate for the questionable benefits or cost of the products.

As beginner runners we try to remember that we're in the sport for the long haul—for better health and fitness over a span of years, not the next meet or race. We should always weigh short-term benefits with long-term gain. Sports drinks, pills and shakes may help us in the short run, but good hydration habits begin and end with simple water.

Cool down and Soreness Tip #2

If ever you feel that you may be too sore for a run, a good rule of thumb is to put on at least one extra layer of clothing, top and bottom (long underwear and a hooded sweatshirt on an average 80 degree day), and attempt your workout at approximately your cool-down pace.

The extra layers will help your sore muscles warm faster to help get you over the "hump" that makes starting a run so difficult and back into your routine when sore. The added sweat and the consequent extra water you will drink should help to flush your system; you should feel good enough to go ahead with your run, if not immediately then the next day.

Be sure, though, not to overheat or ignore warning signals the body might be sending through sore muscles.

Cool down and Soreness Tip #3

Replace a running/workout day with stretching. If you planned to run for, say, 30 minutes, but are feeling sore and beat up, then spend thirty minutes stretching and dynamic stretching, loosening the joints, massaging sore muscles, etc. You may not get the same cardio workout as if you had gone running, but you certainly won't be injured and you're guaranteed to feel better!

As your body gets used to running it will adapt in amazing and wonderful ways, so don't let a little soreness or stiffness slow you down—it's your body's way of telling you it is building muscle and getting into better shape.

Cooling Down Summary

- The goal of a good cool down is oxygen and blood movement throughout the body to promote further circulation and healing for muscles. The only 100% sure way to not have sore muscles is to lessen the intensity of the workout.

- Aim for about 1/5 of workout time to be used for cooling down. If your total warm up and running time was 50 minutes, spend about ten minutes lightly jogging and walking, stretching and loosening the large muscle groups to cool down.

- Transition from full exertion to cooling down gradually, letting your body adjust.

- Think about sore muscles as encouragement—you know that your running is achieving positive results.

- Water, water, water, and then, if you are sore after running, drink more water.

Target Heart Rates

As we begin our initial runs, the only requirement is to be aware of our bodies, our running form, and our breathing. The Training Schedules help to take the guesswork out of what we "should" be doing (of course there's no strict standard to which everyone *must* adhere), and we use this as a guideline to help us feel more comfortable.

Storming out of the house and sprinting up the nearest hill, or trying to run a 10k run our first time out won't help us to achieve long-term goals. Neither will *not* having enough faith in ourselves to persevere when feeling tired or uncomfortable.

The best method for knowing if we are pushing ourselves too hard or not hard enough is to trust our instincts and common sense.

Occasionally, though, we have reason to doubt ourselves or our bodies. Or, we'd like to be a little more precise in our training methods. If this is the case, it's always a good idea to have a working knowledge of our Resting Heart Rate and our Maximum Heart Rate to help determine our Target Heart Rate.

Wearing a heart rate monitor is an easy, accurate method of checking your heart rate. But if you don't have a monitor and don't want to buy one, knowing the basics of our heart rates and how differing heart rates affect us as runners is important information in helping us keep track of our progress, and to know whether or not we are overworking our bodies.

Determining Heart Rate

Our pulse is blood stopping and starting as it moves through the arteries. As children, our resting pulse might range from 90 to 120 beats per minute (BPM), whereas an adult pulse rate slows to an average of 72 beats per minute. As we become fit, however, our resting heart rate should slow to somewhere around 60 beats per minute. Some high-level, elite athletes even have a resting heart rate between 40 and 50 beats per minute.

A lower resting heart rate may indicate that our heart is getting stronger as it is able to pump the same amount of blood at less beats per minute (note that this is a general statement, and is not always the case). The heart is a fantastically muscular organ that pushes blood through a system of blood vessels over 60,000 miles (96,500 km) long! It only makes sense, then, that the stronger and more efficient the heart is, it significantly reduces stress and the chance of heart disease, and helps the body fight off illness.

The easiest place to feel the pulse of a heart beat is the carotid artery in the upper neck area: put your index finger on the side of your neck between the front of your neck and your jaw line. Alternatively, you can also use the radial artery located on the underside of your wrist. Be careful not to use the thumb when checking your pulse, as your thumb has its own pulse and can confuse your count.

You can count the beats for a full 60 seconds or count for 10 seconds and multiply that number by 6. For example, if you felt your heart beat 20 times in 10 seconds the number would be 120 for a full 60 seconds. Counting for only 10 seconds is easier, and a good way to get a quick count during exercise, but to count for the full 60 seconds is more accurate. There are many different ways to achieve the same result, (30 seconds x 2, 15 seconds x 4, etc) but the longer you count the more accurate your reading. Whatever you choose, be consistent in your method as you keep track of your heart rate throughout your training. (Also, be sure to record your resting heart rates in your running journal!). The best time to take your resting heart rate is first thing in the morning, while still lying in bed.

Finding Target Heart Rate: How Hard Should You Train?

To figure out our target heart rate, we must first determine our Maximum Heart Rate (MHR). To do this, subtract your age from 220 for men and 226 for women. (Although this method isn't precise, it gives us a good starting point.) We then use the following formula and exercise zone percentages to arrive at a target heart rate:

MHR – RHR * % + RHR = target heart rate in beats per minute[4]

This is called the Karvonen Method, and although it may look a little mathematical, it's really easier than it looks. Here's a quick example to practice, after you've read about the different exercise zones below.

If my resting heart rate is 60 BPM, my maximum heart rate is 190 BPM, and I want to work out at 75% of my MHR to be squarely in the aerobic zone, then

190-60*.75+60=158 BPM.

So if I want to work for one month at the mid-level of the Aerobic Zone, I will try to focus the majority of my runs to be at about 160 beats per minute, or not quite three times my resting heart rate.

Long, slow runs and easy jogging are usually about 60-70% of MHR – Training in this heart rate zone has two benefits: your heart's ability to pump blood gradually increases, as does the ease of oxygen absorption and delivery, and the muscles' ability to utilize the oxygen improves. Your body also learns to use fat as a source of fuel in this heart rate zone by burning through the readily-accessible energy sources and then tapping into fat storage for fuel. We train our bodies to do this more readily when we exercise consistently. Other benefits include less chance of injury while the same percentage of fat calories is burned as in the more arduous Aerobic Zone (85% of the calories burned for energy come from fat calories in both).[5]

Aerobic Zone 70-80% MHR – The Aerobic Zone is basically the target heart rate. This heart-rate zone is hopefully where most of our training will take place to build cardiovascular fitness. This zone is where you will build up your cardio-respiratory (heart and lungs) capacity so your blood transports oxygen to, and carbon dioxide away from, muscles efficiently.[6]

Aerobic-Lactic Zone 80-90% of MHR—As we become more serious in our running and training, we want to improve our VO2 maximum (the highest amount of oxygen one can consume during exercise). The more oxygen our bodies are able to consume and use efficiently, the longer and harder we can push ourselves. This zone is occasionally called "the lactic threshold" because the muscles build up lactic acid tolerance, which builds endurance and the ability to fight fatigue. Exercise in this zone is difficult but it does improve endurance, strength and performance.[7]

VO2 Max or 'Red Line Zone' – As beginner runners, we really don't concern ourselves with this zone unless we feel that we're reaching 90-100% of our MHR in the first week of the

Training Schedule and so should stop or ease up a bit. This heart rate zone is reserved for the super fit and then only for short periods of time.[8]

Is all this information really practical for beginner runners? In gauging if we are working out hard enough or if we need to push ourselves a little harder, Yes. Even without a heart monitor we can quickly check our pulse at the top of a hill, mid run, or at the end of a run to gauge roughly what zone we're working in and if that zone is sufficient to reach our desired goals. If we're training for a race, for example, we want to largely be working in the aerobic zone, which is where our heart rate would be for most of a race. If our exercise goals are more modest, and we are exercising for general health and well-being, then long, slow, meditative runs would suit our goals better. Monitoring our heart rate helps to keep us interested and motivated in our training as we watch our resting heart rate slow, and our training heart rates become much more efficient!

Determining Target Heart Rate Summary

- We build our heart strength and efficiency just as any other muscle in our body, and the measurement for this is our resting heart rate.

- Knowing the basics about heart rates and training zones will be helpful in ensuring we don't under- or over-train.

- Find your resting heart rate by counting your pulse rate in a 10, 15, or 60 second time period.

- Find your approximate maximum heart rate by subtracting your age from 220 for men and 226 for women.

- To determine your target heart rate, pick the percentage of intensity (thereby the zone) that you want to train in, and use the Karvonen Method (MHR-RHR*%+RHR) to arrive at the target heart rate.

Overtraining and Undertraining: Understanding Session Limits

Concerning whether or not you are training at the right intensity, a lot depends on your level of fitness starting out. You should have probably been a little sore after the first few runs. The body must get used to all of the different muscles and motions used for running, and if you're not sore that's great, but you might ask yourself if perhaps you could have pushed a little harder. (Remembering that as beginner runners we allow ourselves a lot of latitude and a lot of gratitude for just getting out there and getting going!)

Increasing Intensity Tip #1

Use a heart monitor, or take your own pulse mid and/or post-workout. Use the methods described above to determine resting heart rate, maximum heart rate and target heart rate. An elevated heart rate—not too high, not too low—is the best indicator if we are on track in our training.

Increasing Intensity Tip #2

Don't change running times or frequency, but intensity. If we feel it's time to take our training up a notch, we would take the Training Schedule for Non-Exercisers, as an example, and where it says to run and walk in one-minute intervals for a total of 15 minutes, we simply don't alternate the run/walk, but run at an easy pace for fifteen minutes. The next training day, if you are still feeling feisty, then pick up the pace a bit when the Schedule tells you to run/jog for 10 minutes at an *easy* pace, to a slightly quicker pace.

The opposite is also true: if we find that alternating a 15 minute run/walk pace elevates the heart and breathing rate to what we feel are unhealthy levels, then we adjust the Training Schedule to walk briskly for 10 minutes and run/walk for 5. If you notice your resting heart rate rising, chronic or excessive fatigue, frequent illness, or heavy legs, take a rest or slow down your workouts a bit and watch your nutrition particularly closely.

Increasing Intensity Tip #3

As is covered in more detail in Chapter 6, improper nutrition and hydration can give us the same symptoms as overdoing our workouts.

We should always employ common sense as the most important running tool, and use it wisely concerning our training intensity. Consulting a doctor or your running mentor is a good idea if you're not confident about whether you are pushing too hard or not hard enough.

Increasing Intensity Tip #4

Not only do we need to train our bodies gradually, but also our minds. Building self-confidence and healthy running habits are every bit as important as the actual physical benefits of running.

As beginner runners, it's necessary to keep in mind patience, persistence, and moderation. You may feel so good on the endorphin kick of the first few runs that you want to immediately overdo it or jump to a more advanced Training Schedule. Conversely you may feel discouraged by the first few days of training and want to give up. The middle ground of moderation is the way to go for the first few months. At some point in your training you'll want to see how far you can push your body and mind by completing a grueling run, but the first few months of running certainly aren't the time to do this.

Increasing Intensity Tip #5

You won't run consistently if you don't enjoy running. If you are someone who has a very competitive nature and love to push yourself to the limits every time you run—and you can do this and stay healthy—that's great. But, if you find yourself dreading the daily run and making excuses because your training has become too intense, then lighten up—on your runs and yourself. Sticking with your running and not giving up is more important in the long term than risking burnout.

Enjoy yourself as you begin training. Have fun. Listen to your favorite music as you walk and run, go to places you've always wanted to explore, run barefoot around the local ballfield or another grassy area, take your dog or your neighbor's dog . . . and try not to worry too much about weight, times, speed or distance.

Trying to establish a good, strong foundation for your future running, getting to know your body in all of its aspects—mental, physical, breathing—are the main points at this time; whether these initial sessions feel too difficult or too easy, try to stick to the amount of time recommended, while adjusting the pace to your own comfort level.

Aside from conditioning, we are establishing an enjoyable routine, which, if we are persistent enough, our bodies and minds will come to look forward to in the future.

Overtraining and Undertraining Summary

- Only you can really know if you are pushing your body too hard, or not hard enough to reach your goals.

- Using a heart monitor and/or knowing your resting heart rate and maximum heart rate is useful in determining a target heart rate to aim for while running.

- A little soreness is okay as long as it doesn't have an effect on your everyday life.

- Adjust the Training Schedules to be most beneficial for you at the fitness level you are at, but always try to maintain the recommended times.

- No matter what level of fitness, it's a good idea to have a running mentor or be part of a running club to have somewhere to go with specific questions or concerns.

- Use initial runs as a way of developing running as a habit—don't concentrate too much on performance.

- Make your running routine enjoyable by employing as many different tactics as possible.

Visualization #1: The First Run

Begin by sitting in a comfortable chair or couch with your feet on the ground (this symbolizes that we are indeed visualizing, but our feet are still "firmly planted" on the ground) and your hands lying loosely in your lap.

With eyes closed, imagine yourself beginning your run ritual: the pre-run meal, changing into your running clothes, putting on and lacing up your shoes, walking confidently out the door to warm up and start your run. See this process in as much detail as possible, including your warm up routine, and ignore your mind when it becomes impatient.

Next, start down your running path, feeling the ground beneath your feet, hearing your breathing, feeling your arms as they move rhythmically back and forth. You settle into your pace and your breathing levels out; after a few minutes you feel a small twinge of energy as your 'second wind' hits. You pick up the pace gradually, and feel marvelous as your body responds.

Your landmark or halfway point is just ahead and you push your body even faster as you stride through the invisible finish line.

Gradually slowing down to a jog and then a walk, you keep walking, rolling your arms in windmills, bringing your knees to your chest, and drawing deep breaths.

You begin the way home feeling relaxed, confident, and more than a little proud of yourself. The run home is relaxed and fluid; it is by no means easy, but is less intense than the first half of your run. When you arrive back home you take the time to loosen and stretch, being very patient and kind to your body.

You walk back through the door looking forward to some water and maybe a shower, also very much looking forward to tomorrow's run.

Chapter 4: Confidence and Raising the Bar

Confidence and Self-Consciousness

We have decided to start a running regimen to benefit our minds and bodies. Went out and bought a brand new pair of kicks, as the kids say (known as shoes to the rest of us). We have looked at the different Running Schedules and decided which one will work best for us and even decided the day on which we'll start. The snazzy new shorts or sweats are there waiting, right alongside the breathable shirt with more technological advances than most washing machines.

But something holds us back. Perhaps our day to begin comes and goes and we "forgot" to run that morning, or it was too late when we got home from work. We were too busy . . . or maybe, we admit to ourselves, we were scared. Scared we wouldn't be able to run for even ten minutes, or scared how we would look, or scared to take time for ourselves when there is so much to do at work and around the house.

There are legitimate excuses (few, but some) to not begin running, or to miss a day of running, but a lack of confidence or being too self-conscious is never a good reason. Around the country there are loggers and fisherman jogging and running to stay in shape for the upcoming busy seasons, wearing jeans and long-johns to stay warm and looking ridiculous; gawky teenagers running for the next meet; senior citizens staying in shape for their grandkids' sake . . . every shape, size, and speed of runner imaginable.

This is not a psychology text, but suffice to say here that we must be very careful not to project feelings we might have about ourselves onto other people; if we feel overly concerned people aren't supportive, are looking down at us, or are watching our fat jiggle, in all likelihood it's us projecting feelings we have about ourselves onto others. Exercisers in general and runners in particular are some of the friendliest, most supportive folks around, and chances are you will get more than a few encouraging head nods, smiles and comments like, "great job!" whether svelte or obese. Sweat and effort just seem to breed empathy and compatriotism.

Self-consciousness will always affect us to some degree, which is fine as long as we use it to our advantage. We can use self-doubt or self-consciousness as a reminder of why we wanted to begin running and exercising in the first place: for ourselves. Nobody else. We try to always remember two things: one— this ain't no fashion show, and two— the people around us are just as, if not more, self-conscious than we are.

We should remember, too, the positive impact our presence and dedication will have on others. Perhaps a neighbor who has wanted to start exercising will be inspired by our efforts; often the more overweight or out of shape we are, the more inspiring our training becomes.

Or maybe our children learn from us that exercise and taking the time to take care of our bodies is a key family value. Sometimes the time spent running or walking is the only time we get to spend alone with our spouses or loved ones. Ultimately, though, as mentioned in the introduction, we find our own "higher" reason to run and exercise, and we use that reason as a tool to help rid ourselves of doubts and fear.

Overcoming Self-Consciousness Tip #1

Despite a shoe company's admonition to "Just Do it," take your time in preparing for your first runs if you feel self-conscious. Drive or walk the route you will run for several days; know what snack or meal you will eat before and after . . . make every aspect leading up to your running as comfortable as possible so that the actual running becomes an extension of your routine.

Please keep in mind that while running has some immediate benefits, we seek the more enduring rewards of self-confidence, stress relief, and all-around physical health; this means that some initial embarrassment or hesitation is fine, for we know we are trading a few days or weeks of feeling awkward for years of healthy rewards.

Overcoming Self-Consciousness Tip #2

Visualize yourself going on the first few runs. Maybe lying in bed the night before, or throughout the day at work, visualize everything from getting dressed to lacing your shoes, running along your route, and then returning home. See yourself as happy, confident, and accepting of aches, pains, traffic, or whatever else might distract you from enjoying your run.

Overcoming Self-Consciousness Tip #3

If our self-consciousness and fear of running in public is truly debilitating and keeps us from getting started then this, too, is fine. We simply drive, bike or walk to a more isolated place to begin our running.

Overcoming Self-Consciousness Tip #4

If we cannot find a comfortable, private place to run, then we can run on a treadmill or stair-stepper at home until we are confident enough to hit the streets. (Treadmills and other machines are okay, but not as effective in working out the small muscles the variations in trails, paths, and streets provide.) There are often very affordable exercise machines offered at second-hand stores. Occasionally people who are moving out of the area will give away or sell large exercise machines rather than move them. Check your local bulletin boards or Internet lists if this is the route you choose.

Overcoming Self-Consciousness Tip #5

Joining a running club, or finding a few supportive friends for those initial runs will do a lot to dissuade the baseless fears we often create for ourselves. Many people share the same fears and lack of self-esteem; by joining a local running club, or even an Internet group, we can utilize others' experiences and successes to bolster courage. Message boards and online running groups are a great way to remember you're not alone in feeling embarrassed, shy, or hesitant.

No matter what stage we're at in our fitness, there is a runner out there was in exactly the same position at some point in their lives. If you're on a treadmill, but still dreaming of the day you'll be out on the street, contact other athletes to get encouragement and support; write your fears down truthfully in your running journal. Often when we see our fears and prejudices (especially concerning our-selves) on paper, it becomes easier to overcome these phantoms.

Remember to be patient with yourself, but don't wait too long— like standing on the edge of the diving board, the longer we wait the more our minds invent reasons not to take the big plunge.

Finally, if all else fails, put on some good music and run in place at home. This is a surprisingly great way to begin to work on form, breathing, and simply getting used to the motions of running (although the form will be quite a bit different). Wear an extra layer or two of clothing to help get the sweat going, keep those knees up! And have some fun as you build the confidence and discipline in preparation for the "real thing."

Confidence and Self-Consciousness Summary

- Millions of people are out running every day in every shape, shade, and form of clothing imaginable. No matter what we feel or look like, we're not so different from everybody else.

- We often project how we feel about ourselves onto others, and then use others' possible judgment as an excuse not to run.

- We only run for ourselves and our own long-term health and fitness goals.

- If we are too self-conscious to run in public we can:

  Find a more isolated place to run

  Use an exercise machine at home

  Run/walk in place at home

- Join a running club or online chat for support and encouragement.

- Jot down fears in your running journal in order to better deal with them.

Pushing to the Next Level

If you stay dedicated in your running you will peak in your fitness. The good news is that you will more than likely know when you've peaked, generally 6-8 weeks after initially starting out, depending on your fitness level. You will be amazed as your breathing becomes easier to maintain, while distances and times that once seemed far-fetched have now become commonplace. The bad (but exciting) news is that now is the time to take your training up to the next level!

If you haven't seen a fairly dramatic increase in your fitness level, but have diligently followed the Training Schedules, then *usually* the answer is the same: it's time to push your training up to the next level. There are a lot of variables involved in running, of course, but if you haven't seen improvement in speed and endurance, it might be time to give a jolt to what is often referred to as your "muscle memory."

Understanding Muscle Memory

Muscle memory is a very ubiquitous, often overused term, but very important to us as beginner runners. Say we train for several months and build up to about a 9:00 minute-a-mile pace, and then something happens (babies, jobs, injury) and we stop training for six months. We will build back up to that 9:00 minute a mile pace *faster* than someone just starting out because our bodies remember that pace and, most importantly, our bodies (and minds) have the *confidence* in knowing that we can reach and maintain a certain pace.

Muscle memory can be a great advantage, but it can also be a disadvantage if we can't seem to get past a wall, whatever that wall may be: improving a time or pace; not being able to run past the 30 minute mark, for example, or any other running rut in which we are stuck.

As mentioned, muscle memory is a combination of body and mind. If we want to raise the bar and improve our performance, we need to train the muscles to work harder, and to provide support from the nervous system. Just as typing faster becomes a rote activity (we hopefully don't think to ourselves "I will now depress the 'a' key with my left pinky finger"), or catching and throwing a ball becomes automatic, we consciously train, or retrain, our bodies to be able to move faster and farther.

As another example of muscle memory, hiking or climbing a difficult peak may seem impossible. Yet we train and prepare and we eventually climb the peak. Or maybe we don't quite make it. Either way we've pushed ourselves to the point where the next time we climb the mountain or attempt the peak it's less daunting because physically and mentally *we've done this before*, and we have the confidence to know it can be done again.

Whether we are stepping up our training to run a 5K, 10K, a marathon, or just for fun, our training methodology is basically the same. We build foundations for our cardio—breathing and aerobic capabilities—and, almost simultaneously, work in building our endurance and speed musculature until we get to the peak of our fitness.

To sum up, we retrain our muscles by practicing the desired movement, and this recruits better and stronger nervous system connections to those parts. We are better able to perform desired movements smoothly, and it's no surprise on the central nervous system. Once we have pushed to a comfortable point, and then passed that point, we discover a new confidence in our abilities, and the muscles begin to build new "memories" (neural connections) and capabilities.

Understanding Muscle Fibers

To begin improving overall performance, aside from muscle memory, we also need a working knowledge of fast- and slow-twitch muscle fibers. Our slow-twitch muscle fibers are the ones we employ for endurance running, while our fast-twitch muscle fibers are recruited during speed and power bouts.[9] This is a very simplistic explanation, but for our purposes it works; we use both types of muscle fibers for running, and need to build both for improved performance. This is why the Training Schedules alternate between easy, moderate, and fast paces—each help to build speed, endurance, and the mental toughness needed to retrain our bodies.

Combining muscle memory with the slow and fast-twitch muscles, we want to retrain our muscle memory for faster speeds and greater endurance by creating stronger muscles. In this section we'll explore how to improve performance through various training methods, keeping in mind that the mental training, and retraining, is just as important as a training method.

Training Methods for Improving Performance

There are a lot of different ways to do this, and many books have been written solely about this topic, but, arguably, the best and fastest way to see improvement in your running is in running hills.

Hill Running

In whatever form it takes—long and gradual, or short and steep—hill running offers a great way to build the strength of fast-twitch muscles, while also building cardio-vascular (breathing) endurance. You can incorporate hills into your regular routine, or add a hill run or two on top of what you are already running. Whichever you choose, hills should push you deep into the anaerobic activity zone depending on your fitness level. By pushing ourselves up a hill on a regular basis, we retrain our muscles (muscle memory) to rethink what is difficult; we also build endurance by employing fast-twitch muscle fibers to get *up* the hill and our slow-twitch muscles by *continuing to run* after we complete the hill.

The first time we attempt our hill it may be that we have to slow to a walk at the top to recover; hopefully, though, after the first few times we train our bodies to run the hill and then continue on at our regular pace. This trains us to have the mental toughness to push our bodies during "regular" training periods, knowing we will not have to stop or falter to recover.

Running hills are also advantageous in that running uphill isn't as hard on the hip and knee joints as pushing ourselves on flat ground. Running uphill also improves form in that we practice the slight leaning forward of the body, and a flat-footed foot strike while running up an incline has less impact on the lower-leg tendons and joints.

Caution needs to be used on the downhill slopes, however—as we fatigue there is often the tendency to throw our feet in front of our center of gravity using a sharp heel strike to slow down. We don't want to bounce, bound, or jolt while running downhill; we want to keep our balanced foot strike, and use a full body motion that allows us maintain a smooth, fluid form.

Running hills isn't a lot of fun, but it is a great way to improve muscle strength and cardio on the way up, while practicing good form and relaxation techniques as we recover on the way down.

The most important aspect of hill running, whether incorporated into the run, mid-run, or hill repeats, is to *keep moving*.

Maximizing the Benefits of Hill Training

- Hill repeats—Make sure you've done a good 1/3 of your workout before starting hill repeats. Then, approach your hill at normal pace and try to maintain that pace (note the word pace, as in rhythm of the feet, versus speed, to the top of the hill. Try not to stop or slow as you reach the top, but run *through* the crest of the hill. Immediately circle back, jogging lightly back to the bottom, running in a continuous circle. The hill repeats should be about another 1/3 of your workout, while returning to home should be your last third to let your body recover.

- Hill intervals—Similar to hill repeats, with the exception that we break the hill, depending on its length and pitch, into halves or thirds. We approach the hill at our regular pace, and then push ourselves into a sprint for the first half of the hill, and then resume a regular pace through the top of the hill. These are the most difficult hill runs in that we use a lot of energy to sprint through the first half of the hill and then rely on mental toughness and determination to carry us up the second half. After we have done 3-5 of these difficult intervals, we can then switch the order and run the first half of the hill and sprint the second half for 3-5 repetitions.

- Fartlek—So much fun to say, so difficult to do. Similar to intervals, except in a Fartlek hill run we will be alternating our pace every thirty yards or so between a slow jog, run, and sprint, or any combination thereof. We can also decide to run in percentages, saying that we will run the first ¼ of the hill at 30%, the second at 80%, and the remaining half at 50 % of our full capacity, for example.

The Fartlek accomplishes several things, not the least of which is to teach us that we are indeed in control of the pace we run, and have choices in our speed and breathing. The Fartlek helps to build mental discipline as much as it helps to build muscle and aerobic capacity. The difference between intervals, repeats and Fartleks is the unstructured nature of Fartleks; they can be incorporated anywhere, at anytime during a run. Although they are designed with racers in mind, (Fartlek means "speed play" in Swedish) to keep an opposing runner from passing us by speeding up dramatically, it is also very useful to us beginner runners.

Explosive runs up a hill followed by a full-body collapse

do not help us in long-term training goals. As mentioned, even if we have to slow to a walk at the top of the hill or walk back down the hill as we recover, we need to keep the blood and oxygen flowing and maintain an elevated heart rate.

We may look like one of the early stages of evolution as we reach the top of the hill, but we don't give up, and we keep our arms moving, even when our legs feel like lead.

Often it is our minds, not our bodies, that tell us, "If I push myself to pass this person I won't be able to keep running . . . if I attempt this hill too fast it will hurt and I'll have to stop." The old adage that "the mind is willing but the body is weak" is turned on its head in running. It is the mind that gives us doubts and tells us that our bodies hurt or are too tired to continue.

If we want to truly improve our performance, mental toughness and ignoring the little voice of doubt is a vitally important step. Other runners, remember, have all been at these initial stages of doubt and faltering discipline; we must have tenacity and enjoyment in our routine, and then, gradually, we become stronger both physically and mentally.

Improving Performance Tip #1

All of the methods described above for hill running can, and should, be incorporated at some point in your regular routine. The Training Schedules already incorporates intervals for maximum benefit during the training week, but as we mature as runners we can tweak intensity to suit our needs.

Improving Performance Tip #2

Once our running routine has become habit, any cross-training exercises such as stairs or bleachers are a good addition to running. By incorporating different strength-building exercises into our regular running schedule, we are able to build peripheral muscles for support and balance, or focus on other areas where we need more strength or agility.

Plyometrics, where wooden boxes are used to lightly step and jump onto, are a great way to build fast-twitch muscle. Everyday objects such as chairs, or a sturdy coffee table can also be used: place the chair or table against a wall to ensure it doesn't slide, and then step onto it and back down, alternating legs, going as quickly (and safely!) as possible. Plyometrics helps with strengthening the core, glutes, calves, lower legs, and overall agility.

Improving Performance Tip #3

Improving running performance includes increasing stride length and stride rate. This is a paradoxical topic, but essentially we are not trying to reach out further and over-stride, but instead increase "air time" between footfalls. Increasing stride length, in this case, means creating more distance between foot strikes; depending on different variables such as fitness level and the length of your legs, this may mean actually *shortening* your stride!

In our initial runs we "stepped out" a little to increase flexibility and to help keep the alignment of our bodies. Now, we are working on lengthening our stride through the improved strength in our legs and feet by *shortening* our stride but increasing the number of strides in a given distance.

Confused? Think of it like this: given a specific distance: we run this distance at our normal pace. We then run the distance again, increasing the cadence, (or number of foot falls) to discover that our stride (length) is the same or has increased slightly (but we ran the same distance, faster!) A good runner will generally be around 90 steps per minute employing fairly quick, efficient strides.

We still want to be conscious of good form: we are not suddenly sprinters bringing our knees higher or pumping the arms more. We maintain a good economy of movement and balance by keeping our legs and feet under our center of gravity. As with everything in running, this should be done gradually and gracefully.

Having a smooth, long stride without compromising good form depends a lot on the strength of the body, both upper and lower. The best way to increase the explosive power needed to increase stride length? Hills, of course. Bleachers, plyometrics, and step-ups will work, but by far the fastest way to see improvement in the explosive power needed for increased stride length and stride rate is to run hills.

Improving Performance Tip #4

To be strong runners, we need a strong core. It is an absolute myth that running is "mostly lower body." The core is usually defined as the upper body excluding limbs, but as runners we should include the biceps because the arms play such a crucial role in good running form.

We improve our core when running hills, or alternating speeds and pace because we work different muscle groups than when we are running on flat ground for extended periods of time. Both have their place in our running routine, but we need to be careful to keep them balanced and not favor one over the other.

Another way to improve our core strength is crunches, wherein we lie on our back with feet crossed in the air and the knees at a 90 degree angle to the floor. With the hands near the ears, we bring our elbows to meet our knees. Thirty to sixty crunches before and/or after a run will truly help with endurance, aches, pains and good core strength. Gradually build up to as many crunches as you can, even if you can do only five or so starting out.

There are a million and one different ways to strengthen the core, but for us the main concept is that if our lower back is sore from running, for example, this can be generally attributed to weak stomach muscles. By building the core, we bring all of the disparate but connected parts of the body together in a strong center.

Ultimately, the core is the entire trunk of our body and we need to maintain a good strong balance in our core to keep everything else functioning properly.

Improving Performance Tip #5

Disassociate the mind from the body. Very Zen, right? Not really. This is a very practical way to make sure we don't let short-term worries interfere with our long-term health and well-being.

A common scenario would be that we are set to run for 40 minutes in week 15 of a Training Schedule, yet at the 30 minute mark we begin to think, "Ah, if I turned around now I would still have time to finish that report before dinner . . . I think my right leg is aching a bit, I'd better turn around . . .

Oh, I hate leaving the house such a mess while I'm running."

Sound familiar?

When that little voice begins to sound, we acknowledge it but don't give it any credence. We might say, "Ah, there's my mind again, trying to get me to do less than I could and should. Funny little voice. Listen to it jabber on and on while I continue my run . . ."

The same is also true with our bodies. If we *identify* with our aches and pains instead of simply acknowledging them and moving on, we allow the minor details of our lives control over our goals and choices.

For example, at some point in running we will feel as if each of our legs is filled with lead and we aren't able to take another step. If we identify with our legs, we say to ourselves, "My legs feel like lead. I am completely exhausted. I have to stop." If we employ disassociation we say, "Those legs feel heavy. That's interesting, last week they got this feeling at the 25 minute mark and it's now past the 30 minute mark. My body must be getting stronger . . ." Just because one part of our body, or schedule, or life, is weary, busy, or otherwise full of angst, does not mean we have to compromise our fitness and running goals.

Again, this is not a philosophy or psychology text, but the ability to separate ourselves from the body and the doubting mind is a basic tenet of any athlete, but particularly runners where we often don't have the luxury of coaches and teammates.

Improving Performance Summary

- Run Hills. No matter in what form or shape they come in, hills are great for mental and physical endurance, increased strength, and cardiovascular capacity.

- Use variations in speed and pacing to work on both fast- and slow-twitch muscle fibers. This *doesn't* mean making your running erratic or full of stop/start motions. But *do* give your body the opportunity to be able to change speed and pacing without causing undue stress.

- Work on stride length by increasing pace or your foot strike rate, always remembering to "stay on top of your feet," meaning you still maintain a good, balanced running form.

- Maintain and work on a strong core. Whether hip flexors, abdominals or lower back, our core, front and back, does a lot for overall health.

- Keep our minds and bodies in check by disassociation. We don't allow little worries, aches, or pains to keep us from reaching our full potential.

Chapter 5: Staying Motivated

There are as many *kinds* of running as there are runners, and one way to stay motivated and keep running enjoyable is to explore the many different types of running available. This can include "hashing," which is generally running around drinking beer as fast you can run (and drink) through a set course, to joining in competitive events and/or fun runs for various causes.

On a less extreme level, we can keep ourselves interested by varying our routines, whether by changing the time of day we run, the distance and/or intensity, or the route. There are many exercise machines and new running shoes at second-hand stores attesting to the fact that many people start out with good intentions only to let procrastination and lack of motivation get in the way of their goals.

No matter how far-fetched or silly the idea may be, if it keeps you running then do it. Run to the coffee shop for a coffee before returning home. Have someone take your things to work for you while you run to work. Put a dollar or two in a jar every time you run. Allow yourself a good sugary food, like a donut, after you run (not recommended for weight loss, of course, but still a good motivator). The bottom line is we intuitively know what's healthy, what's good for the mind and body, and what will keep us running. If the occasional jelly donut every week or so is your reward, then go for it!

Only a lack of imagination can keep you from running! Be inventive, make up your mind to make running an integral part of your life, and commit yourself to a lifestyle centered around your own well-being.

Motivation Tip #1

Listen to inspirational music, news or other pro-grammed material.

This not only helps us to look forward to running, but it also adds to the idea we aren't "losing time" while running. With today's portable devices, we can brush up on world events, hear motivational talks, or listen to a great book, thereby combining multiple joys of life!

There are also specialized sites wherein one can down-load music that is specifically meant for running purposes. Thirty or sixty seconds of material, for example, are helpful in interval runs so we don't have to check our watches, or try to keep track in our minds.

Motivation Tip #2

Be in a supportive community of runners and be sup-portive of yourself. This means putting as much effort into running as you do into other parts of your life. Be as supportive of yourself and your running as you are of other people and their activities.

Have the kids make their own lunch in the mornings, join a carpool so you don't have to drive as much, and make sure your immediate family and friends know of your com-mitment to running and exercise. Once we have established running as part of our persona these things become second nature, but as we begin running we need people who will encourage us to pursue our running goals.

Some of us are less intrinsically motivated than others. And there will always be days, no matter how motivated we are, when we feel more like drooling in front of the television than getting out and running.

On these days it is invaluable to have someone to call and give us one of those annoyingly righteous pep talks that get us out of the house and moving.

Motivation Tip #3

We burn around 100 calories a mile when we run, depending on the speed in which we run, our size, terrain, etc. There are many tables and charts online to help you figure out more precisely how many calories you burn over distance and time. The bigger you are, the more calories you burn. A 130 pound person will burn about 650 calories if they run at a 9 minute mile pace for an hour, while a 180 pound person will burn about 900 calories if also running at the same pace and amount of time.

So we don't want to negate the difficult runs we're doing by eating a lot of high-calorie, low-nutrition foods. Not only does stuffing our face with potato chips give us hard-to-burn empty calories, it also keeps us from building the muscle that will later burn calories while are resting. We not only increase calorie intake, but also lose the metabolism to burn those calories on a daily basis.

Take home message? Take breaks from running as a part of training, but not simply because you don't want to train or don't feel like it. It's fine to take a day to "sharpen the saw," get rested up, eat well, stretch, and prepare for the next day's workout. We should never feel guilty about taking a day for our bodies. But there are days, and there *will* be days, when we know that we *need* to go on a run for our physical and mental well being (and maybe for the well being of those around us!) and we procrastinate. Make excuses. Find terribly urgent things to do such as clip our fingernails or bake apple turnovers. This is dangerous territory because it leads to inconsistency. Inconsistency leads to a little guilt, and a little guilt goes a long way. Finally, we become disgusted with our program and ourselves because we're not seeing results, and ironically enough, we give up.

Motivation Tip #4

Set reasonable and attainable goals and reward yourself when you achieve them. Record these goals in your running journal, and as you visualize remind yourself of your goals and why they are important to you.

Setting short-term goals— Just getting out, following the Training Schedules, and running for five days a week is a worthy goal, and achievement, in and of itself. You might tack on eating one healthier meal a day, or cutting out one soda or fast food meal per day or week. Then, when you achieve these small goals, reward yourself by downloading some new tunes on your music player, buying yourself some new shoes, or going to a spa. Or, less expensively, cook a nice meal for yourself and a friend, or just watch a movie with popcorn (and butter, because you've earned it!).

You should have specific goals, but be careful of goals involving times and weights, such as, "I'll make it to the third mailbox under forty minutes by the end of the month, and I'll have lost ten pounds," or, "I'll have my blood pressure down in two months . . ."

Our beginning goals should be oriented more toward discipline, making running a daily habit, and the mental aspects of running; things we have direct control over, not end results and short-term achievement.

There is absolutely nothing wrong with setting our sights on losing weight or trying to run faster and farther, but our bodies are such dynamic, unreliable things that resting our motivational hopes on them doesn't make a lot of sense. We want short-term goals that lend themselves to long-term goals that in turn stretch out for years.

We want to make commitments to ourselves that are sustainable no matter what weight we're at, or want to be, and no matter how fast or slow we can run.

Setting Long-term goals— Set yourself to running in a race. It doesn't really matter the length or event, but running with other runners and being "selfish" enough to take the time and energy in reaching a goal is a great way to show that you're serious about running and staying healthy.

Set your sights on a race far enough in the distance that you must train diligently for it for quite some time. Try not to enter a race three weeks away and train like a fiend—this could lead to burnout and only a short-term gain. Remember we want achievable, *sustainable* goals— particularly long-term goals—that will keep us running and competing for years, not months.

Set both personal and private long-term goals— We really shouldn't set goals for anyone other than ourselves and our own health, but if we tell a friend that we'll run with him or her three times a week, then we are more likely to be motivated to go than if we are only going by ourselves. The same holds true for races or events—we're more likely to train for a marathon or half marathon if we've bought the plane tickets, or have a firm commitment to run with someone, or if we've signed up for the race and paid our money.

Motivation Tip #5

Take before, during and after photos. Just as you keep track of times and distances in your running journal, take time to post photos there of yourself as you progress in your fitness. It is often difficult to see ourselves objectively without photos, so we use these as reminders of both how far we've come and how far we need to go.

Motivation Tip #6

Use visualization time to see yourself becoming motivated. If you are having trouble getting off the couch, visualize yourself overcoming inertia, getting dressed for running and heading out the door. Use this time to think about how good you'll feel after the run, and the pride that comes from taking care of your body.

The common excuses, "I don't have time . . . the dishes are piled up in the sink . . . I just really don't feel like running today," may all be somewhat valid excuses, but they are still excuses. Use visualization and short meditation times to cut through the excuses. In the end we will always find that these excuses we use are tantamount to saying: "I don't find my personal health as important as my commitments to other people and things."

If we schedule running every day and make it as ordinary as brushing our teeth, we will find that the sense of accomplishment that comes from having a healthy habit will far outweigh the minor disruptions in our schedules caused from making time to run.

Motivation Tip #7

When you *really* don't feel like running, take a deep breath and say, "Okay, I'll run today, but then I'll take tomorrow off." This is a bit of a lie, of course, for we will say the same thing the next day.

The lesson here is to occasionally not think too far ahead or behind, or the goals in the distance not yet met, but just focus on the workout for that day. Sometimes it's enough to say, "I'll just get my gear on and walk to the mailbox, but that's it." Once outside and moving, chances are we'll go ahead with our run.

Staying Motivated Summary

- Vary routines in distance, time, intensity, and location.

- Listen to music, news, inspirational, or motivational material while running.

- Surround yourself with people who are supportive of your goals and, more importantly, support yourself with the time and space needed to achieve your goals.

- Take breaks from your running when you feel you need them *as part of your training schedule.* Rest and recovery is a very important and often overlooked part of training, but you don't want to become inconsistent in your running and training.

- Set reasonable, attainable and sustainable goals, both short-term and long-term.

- Use visualization exercises to help get you up off of the couch and out running. Visualize what you want to look and feel like in six months time, and how you will achieve that. Chances are it won't involve skipping another workout!

- Take it one day at a time. This is another of those paradoxes: to achieve long-term goals we sometimes need to focus on the small, small picture of just getting out and running *that day.*

- Whatever works for you works! Whatever method, reward, or strategy you employ, even if it involves jelly donuts, is better than not running at all.

Visualization #2: Staying Strong

On this day your body feels great. Not only do your legs not turn to lead in the first ten minutes of your run; your stomach, chest and arms feel strong and tight. The first ten minutes of the run seem to fly by before you've even noticed, and the first big hill is looming in front of you. You feel yourself leaning into the hill and meeting the hill without any hesitation. Your lungs burn a little as you climb the hill, but you keep pumping and churning. At the top of the hill you are exhausted but you can also feel the excitement of the hard run, and you make yourself continue on. To your surprise your breath returns quickly and you are able to continue on running at a smooth, comfortable pace.

You allow a small grin as you realize that from this point on you will always be a runner, gaining strength and confidence every single time you run.

Chapter 6: Nutrition and Hydration

These are suggestions only, to give an idea of good eating habits while running and training. The best rule for eating before running is to be neither full nor hungry. Post-run eating suggestions are similar, with perhaps a little more protein and smaller portions. The quick meals listed below have a morning (AM) run in mind, but they can work for an afternoon or evening workout as well.

Changing our diet and exercise routines to become more fit seems natural, yet this also seems to be the very reason so many of us lose our resolve after starting a new program: trying to do too much at once. If you can change both at once then great, make a fresh start and keep on going! But many of us need a gradual change, and just starting an exercise routine is plenty to keep us busy.

So we can focus on our running, and still maintain our usual diet but change it gradually. We can still have our cheeseburgers, but we take off the bun and the mayonnaise, thereby saving almost five hundred calories; still have a peanut butter sandwich, but on whole grain bread with no-sugar peanut butter, etc. A good nutritious diet is one that fits easily into your life and budget—not one that promises miracles in thirty days and causes you to take out a second mortgage! Just like running, our nutrition goals should be attainable *and*, most importantly, sustainable.

In the beginning, eat the same foods and the same meals as you normally would, but try to switch out or leave out one or two things at every meal. Too often exercise and diet programs promise great dramatic results, but we *are* creatures of habit. We end up not sticking with it *because* it is so great and dramatic, but perhaps not in a way that works or is right for us.

Short 15-30 Minute Run Pre-Run Meals and Snacks. Eat 30-40 minutes before a run.	Long (30-60 minute run) Pre-Run Meals. Eat 40-60 minutes before a run.
Oatmeal	Oatmeal with one or two eggs, scrambled, hard-boiled or poached
Dry toast with peanut butter	Buttered toast with peanut butter and banana
Crackers with peanut butter	Crackers with slices of avocado and tomato
Sliced apple with peanut butter	Oatmeal with apple and peanut butter
Half a bar of chocolate with a banana	Small to medium plate of spaghetti (6-10 oz.) or other pasta with light sauce
Small bowl of pasta, with little or no sauce	Rice and beans
Small bowl of rice, with or without beans, chicken or other meat.	Baked potato with butter and cheese
Tossed green salad with light dressing	Tossed green salad with toast or crackers
Yogurt with almonds or other nuts	Yogurt with almonds or other nuts, raisins, and a piece of lunchmeat or other meat
Quesadilla with whole wheat or corn tortilla	Fajitas with whole wheat or corn tortillas

Carbohydrates

As runners, our diets should consist of about 60% carbohydrates, or carbs, as they are commonly called. These include most pastas and rice, and sugars most readily found in fruits and, yes, candy. Our bodies burn carbs more easily than just about any other food because of the ease that carbohydrates turn into glucose, which is the sugar that feeds our energy needs.

Carbohydrates are often blamed as a weight gainer, and this is partly true—if you eat a lot of carbs, which then turn to sugar, and don't burn that sugar through expended energy you can gain weight. But as runners we need the fuel carbohydrates provided to get the maximum benefit from our workouts.

Some people may have to cut out carbs almost altogether to lose weight. If you have been running diligently and haven't noticed a decrease in weight, this may be your situation, which means you might have to replace the carbohydrates in your diet with more nuts (protein) and fruits for good nutrition.

There are two types of carbohydrates: simple and complex. The simple carbs consist of most of our junk foods such as candy and soda, but also fruits. Eating an apple or an orange before or after a run to replenish glucose is a great quick energy boost, not to mention the added benefit of vitamins and fiber fruit provides that candy and other simple carbs don't.

There is certainly a place for simple carbs in our diets when we are working out a lot—some people run into problems, though, when a large portion of their diet consists of these quick, sugary meals. Simple carbs provide a great boost to our energy, but the energy provided is short lived and liable to lead to a real hunger, wherein we gorge ourselves. A little sugar before or after a run isn't a bad idea, but it should never exceed about 10% of the total 60% of the carbs we need. A majority of the rest of the carbs should come from complex carbohydrates.

Complex carbohydrates consist of foods such as pasta, breads, vegetables and rice. Because complex carbs can be concocted and cooked in so many ways, incorporating them into your diet shouldn't be a problem. Be careful to eat as much unprocessed, whole-grain products as possible, and pastas and breads without the added sugar. It is always surprising how many products—bread, hamburger and hot dog buns, pasta sauces—that seem so innocuous have a large amount of sugar and preservatives added to them. Like any other machine, we want our bodies running on the best, cleanest fuel possible.

Fats

Fats should make up about 20% of our diets, or daily calorie intake, with saturated fats such as red meat and dairy products comprising, at the most, about 10%. Try to keep in mind the three different forms of fat, from worst for us to best: saturated (red meat, dairy), poly (margarine and butter alternatives) and mono (natural oils and dressings). Saturated fats are usually solid in form, while mono-saturated fats are almost always liquid. This is why fish oil, for example, is well known as a great way to feed our bodies "good" fat.

Again, for maximum benefit to our bodies, these fats, especially the oils used for cooking, butter, or margarine, should be as unprocessed as possible.

Is real butter, then, a better choice than low-calorie butter? Yes, as long as we are expending that extra energy real butter provides by running, rather than slathering real butter on our toast and then sitting in our office chair all day. There are also low-calorie alternatives that are not substitute products, or over-processed. The key is only allowing solid fats (saturated) to take up a small portion of our daily diets and/or daily caloric intake.

Proteins

Protein helps to build and repair muscles and tendons, and so should be an integral part of our training diets, comprising about 20%. Eggs, fish, meat and beans are all good sources of protein, as long as we keep in mind the amount of saturated fats contained in red meat. As runners, nuts and beans are some of the best options, while, contrary to popular belief, protein bars and shakes are some of the worst. Why? Because protein bars and shakes are condensed versions of nutrition, which our bodies have trouble metabolizing and digesting smoothly. On race day, or on a particularly difficult training day, one, or the other isn't a terrible option, but we shouldn't place our nutritional needs on products or pills.

Some of these nutritional needs and requirements can get confusing, but they can be kept simple. For example, a bowl of rice and beans with some olive oil is essentially the perfect meal: the rice satisfies our carb requirement, the beans our protein, and the oil our fat. We can add a little fish to this, scrambled eggs, or vegetables. Eating simply, in other words, doesn't have to be complicated, dull, or expensive. We just have to watch out for processed foods, especially fats, and remember the percentages 60/20/20 for carbohydrates, fats, and proteins.

Listen to your intuition while training and running, and your body will usually tell you what you need to be eating. If you are craving sugar and chocolate after runs, start incorporating more "good" fat into your diet. If you are feeling weak, sore and beat up after runs, try adding more beans, fish, or other sources of protein.

Starving ourselves to lose weight or look better will only lead to injury, decreased performance on runs and ultimately a feeding frenzy of bad food. As runners we need to feed and hydrate our bodies consistently and gradually; eating a healthy snack and guzzling water an hour before or after a run isn't adequate.

If we allow it, good nutrition can become an enjoyable habit just as much as our running, which, when combined, becomes a lifestyle change that betters our health, energy levels, and mental health.

Hydration

Our bodies need a lot of water. Our total physical makeup is approximately two-thirds water, and when we run we lose water through the cooling process of evaporation (perspiration). Drinking water before and after a run helps, of course, but not as much as a constant and consistent intake of water.

The old adage to drink eight, eight-ounce glasses of water a day works fairly well as a baseline, but this varies widely with body type and environment. If you feel thirsty during or after a run, then you probably are not hydrating properly in the hours in between. When our bodies send the signal that we're thirsty, it's usually too late to really have good hydration. In other words, don't drink water only when thirsty, but instead make it a regular part of your day. In theory, your body shouldn't ever have to tell you it needs water, especially if we're running and training a lot.

Sports drinks are good ways to replenish fluids, and if you are able to drink more fluids because of them then go for it. But there are many wild-land firefighters and other emergency personnel who can attest to the fact that over-reliance on sports drinks can lead to heat stroke and severe dehydration. Drinks such as Gatorade have an astounding amount of sugar in them, which is handy for a quick boost of energy, but over time the amount of sugar triggers the stress response in the body, much like too much caffeine, and acts as a diuretic, or increased urination.

There are several better ways to make water tasty while replenishing your body's water and electrolyte needs: a simple glass of water with a *small amount* of salt and pure cane sugar works just as effectively as a sports drink; you can also add some fruit juice, honey, lime or lemon to replace the sugar or as flavoring. There are also several companies who make small packets of flavoring for flavored water that taste great without the added sugars, dyes, preservatives, and other unneeded additives.

Nutrition and Hydration Summary

- Take it slow. Many people find changing both exercise and diet overwhelming, so establish your running routine first, and then gradually change your diet. Exchanging foods or leaving out portions of our regular diets is a great way to start a new diet plan.

- Keep it simple. Our bodies need carbohydrates, fats, and proteins. When we eat all of these in moderate amounts (60/20/20) and keep our food as basic and unprocessed as possible, we will feel and see the positive results.

- Eating healthy doesn't have to be a dramatic change to our pocketbooks or lifestyle.

- Sports and energy drinks are great for every-once-in-a-while use, but not as a substitute for good, consistent nutrition and hydration.

- We want to develop habits that are sustainable for years, not a fad to be tried and discarded in months.

Chapter 7: Running in Adverse Conditions, and Common Injuries

Adverse Weather Considerations

Snowing and blowing outside? A hundred degrees in the shade? Whatever the weather, with a little forethought and planning, we should be able to run in it. We never want to chance hurting ourselves by sliding on icy slopes or developing heat stroke, yet at the same time we want as many opportunities to get out on the road as humanly possible.

As with all of running, running in less-than-ideal weather means knowing your limitations and capabilities. Endangering ourselves for the sake of exercise isn't a good idea, but neither is letting a little weather get in our way. We don't want to add any helpful excuses to our list!

We should always remember to wear bright clothing, even in good weather, to be seen easily, but especially when it's grey outside, at evening or dusk. There are many products to help us be seen by motorists that are easy to find and affordable; blinking lights, and reflective strips on clothing and shoes are good ideas when running in reduced visibility.

If you have any reservations about the conditions in which you'll be running, make a plan for reduced runs until you're more acclimated and feel more comfortable about the weather. Try not to run for "personal bests" in extreme weather; keep training and wait for a better time when there's less risk.

In hot or cold weather it's always a good idea to let

people know the route you are going to run and the estimated time you'll be returning. That way if there are problems someone can quickly cover your route and find you if there happens to be an issue.

As runners, diversity is our friend. This is not "old school" thought along the lines of, "what doesn't kill you makes you stronger," but rather a fact in that the more our bodies have to adapt to changing conditions, the stronger and more confident we become. This is why going to a gym and running on a treadmill isn't listed as one of the ways to deal with adverse weather. Sure, it is a viable option, but running on a treadmill simply doesn't take the mental toughness and physical awareness that running in "the weather" does.

We don't do anything in running out of stubbornness or bravado, but only what will benefit us most in the long run (no pun intended). There is a certain strength, vitality, and versatility that comes with running outdoors, in all kinds of different conditions, that a treadmill just can't offer. Plus, many runners find that their times improve when running in hot or cold weather!

Hot Weather Considerations

Hot Weather Tip #1

When running in hot weather, always carry as large a water bottle as is comfortable with you while running. Drinking water along the way and being able to spritz or spray water helps to keep the body's core temperature cool.

Another good way to keep water with us is to have little water caches at different points along the route. It only takes a few minutes beforehand to place water in discreet places, and icy-cold water waiting for you at the next stop makes for a great motivator on a hot day!

If ever you feel like your body is no longer producing sweat, and you feel dizzy, disoriented, or lightheaded, immediately stop running as these are signs of heatstroke.

Hot Weather Tip #2

A comfortable, broad-brimmed hat will help keep the sun off the head and face, and loose-fitting, synthetic shirts and shorts are best for running in hot weather. Also remember to wear a sweat-proof sunscreen, but don't put it on your forehead as your sweat will mix with the sunscreen and run into your eyes, making for a very blurry and painful run.

Hot Weather Tip #3

If the weather is humid and hot, take a running towel along with you to wipe off the sweat to allow the body to "condensate" more freely. Similar to the effect of jumping into a hot shower immediately after a run, hot humid weather doesn't allow the body to cool itself through con-densation (sweat) because the skin is already saturated. Drying the face and arms during a humid run will help to alleviate this and help to keep the body's core temperature cooler. During hot, dry weather a cold, wet running towel around the neck is also a good idea.

Hot Weather Tip #4

Common sense tells us, too, that if we know it's going to be hot then running in the early mornings or late evenings is a great way to beat the heat. These are also great times to have a little more space, to vary routine, and to watch the sunrise or sunset!

Cold Weather Considerations

Cold Weather Tip #1

The general rule of thumb in running in cold weather is to wear one less layer than you think necessary. Many runners, however, like to keep extra layers on during cold weather to induce and maintain a good sweat. No matter what your personal preference, the important thing to remember is to keep the big muscles of your legs and glutes covered with tights or long johns (with sweats or shorts over them!), and layered long-sleeved shirts for the upper body. A light, loose anorak, which is a pullover jacket, is great for running because the generated body heat stays trapped against the torso, while allowing for freedom of movement.

As with hot weather, synthetic fabrics are better than natural fabrics for wicking moisture away from the body. The exception to this is silk, which is a great fabric for hot and cold weather and can be obtained affordably from most outdoor sports stores.

Always take particular care of the extremities—nose, ears, fingers, toes—and follow mom's advice about heat loss through the head— wear a good warm hat!

Cold Weather Tip #2

Carry a jacket or pullover that packs into itself and can easily be stowed in a fanny pack or carried in your hand when you get too hot. If running in a remote area, you can hang your extra jacket on a tree or post to grab on the return trip.

Remember, though, to be careful about getting hot quickly, shedding extra layers, and then being too exposed to a cold wind or sudden flurry of snow. It's always better to be a little warm and sweating than to be sweating and freezing at the same time, with your extra clothing two miles back down the road, or not enough clothing.

Cold Weather Tip #3

You may experience a feeling like your lungs are "burning" when first running in cold weather. This will probably go away after a week or so as your lungs become acclimated, but if it doesn't there are a couple of things you can try. Breathing in through your nose and out of your mouth allows for more humid air to reach the lungs; wearing a light scarf or balaclava also helps to humidify the air. The simplest option is a piece of gum, which keeps your mouth moist and can help to "soften" the cold, dry air before it reaches the lungs.

Cold Weather Tip #4

Continue to maintain good hydration. A cold wind can dehydrate your body just as fast as a warm or hot wind, so remember to drink plenty of fluids. Your fluid diet may change a bit from cold water to warm tea or warm drinks, but whatever the form or temperature of your liquids, maintain good hydration habits.

Wet Weather Considerations

Wet Weather Tip #1

The most difficult part about running in wet weather is running in wet weather! But don't let the rain stop you—dress in layers, following the same guidelines as in cold weather, with a base layer of polypropylene or other synthetic material, followed by loose outer garments that can be easily removed. Synthetic materials wick away moisture faster than most natural materials, and so stay lighter and dryer when worn. Don't make the mistake, however, of thinking that more layers means staying dryer. In wet weather more layers usually just means more wet clothes.

Wet Weather Tip #2

Wear a hat to help keep water off your face and out of your eyes. Any kind of hood, though, usually constricts vision and traps heat, causing you to be more uncomfortable from sweat than you would from the rain!

Wet Weather Tip #3

The same goes with a waterproof jacket or slicker—these usually cause more sweat and constriction than they're worth. A loose windbreaker or anorak is a better option. Generally speaking, loose outer layers in wet weather work better than form-fitting clothing to shed water and keep from over-heating.

Remember to wipe the mud and water from your shoes after your run. Then, remove the insoles and set them out to dry. Stuff newspaper or paper towels inside the shoes to absorb the remaining moisture.

No matter what the weather, wear bright, reflective clothing. Lights and other running-specific gadgets are needed when running in inclement weather or at night.

You don't always have to wear running-specific clothing, but wear what is most comfortable and safe for the conditions in which you are running. A person can easily spend a thousand dollars on a running gear, but the best running outfit will *always* be the one you're wearing while you run.

Adverse Weather Conditions Summary

Hot Weather Considerations

- Carry water with you or create water caches

- Loose, light clothing

- Evaporation and condensation—carry a hand towel and use it.

- Wet towel around the neck

- Run early in the morning or late in the evening.

- Know the dangers and warning signs of heat stroke.

- Don't go for personal bests on dog days.

- Be visible!

Cold Weather Considerations

- Layers, layers, layers – and safe places to shed them or put them back on.

- Wear less than you think you need, but remember sweat is your friend.

- Lung pain and burning will usually stop after a week or so. If it doesn't, try the methods listed.

- Be careful to cover extremities such as fingers, ears and nose in severe cold.

- Hydration is still extremely important, particularly in cold, windy conditions.

- Be visible!

Wet Weather Considerations

- Wear breathable, wickable material in your base layer.

- Don't constrict body heat with a slicker or raincoat as it will cause more moisture than the rain.

- Be visible!

Common Running Injuries and Treatment

At some point in our running careers, whether competitive or hobbyist, we will get sore muscles, achy joints, and tender tendons. Of course if we train gradually and take care of our bodies, these injuries and ailments should be kept to a minimum.

On a scale of 1 to 10, with 10 being an injury that requires time off from running and 1 being completely healthy, most running injuries rate about a 5. Sometimes these middle-of-the-road injuries simply need an ice pack or a heat bath, while others seem to persist no matter what we do and so become more aggravating than a "serious" injury. While these types of injuries are usually more annoying than dangerous, they can still take the enjoyment out of our running and cause us to lose motivation.

Many of these nagging injuries will heal over time as our muscles become stronger and used to working with each other in different ways, others may have to be dealt with by seeing a specialist. Each individual runner will have to decide what the trigger point is in deciding when to seek professional help regarding an injury. Being proactive through good warm-up, cool-down, nutrition and hydration is by far the best way to prevent running injuries from ever occurring.

Listed below are some common injuries to runners. As you read them, think about what you've read so far in this book and try to decide what may be the underlying cause for the injury: poor running form, core strength imbalance, nutrition, or improper hydration. *Almost* all injuries are a result of one, or a combination of, these factors.

Runner's Knee[10]

This is, aptly, the most common running injury. Runner's knee is characterized by pain just below or behind the kneecap, with lingering soreness after sitting for long periods of time.

Treatments:

- Shorten your stride to lessen the impact and strain on the knees.

- Run up hills to lessen impact, while also building the quadriceps and other leg muscles that help to keep knees moving correctly. Walk or go slower down hills to lessen the jolt and strain on the knees.

- Ice your knees after running when you first feel pain coming on, and use a heat pad to warm your knees before and after running as the condition improves.

- Loosen your knees throughout the day, especially when sitting.

- Try to run off of asphalt or hard-packed dirt and track; if at all possible, find a trail, sandy beach or grassy area to run on.

Conditions:

Shorten the amount of time and distance in your runs. If your knees are not feeling better in about a week's time, or you are feeling twinges of knee pain at the insides or outsides of your knees, then you need to stop running to let the tendons heal. If you are only feeling pain at the beginning of your runs, after sitting, or going down stairs, then you can probably keep training to strengthen the knee. Remember that persistent knee pain can mean taking a little preventative time off now, or a lot of recovery time taken off later.

Plantar Fasciitis[11]

Symptoms:

Pain on the underside of the foot in the tendons that run from the heel to the toes. This is sometimes referred to as a "stone bruise," or occasionally mistaken for heel (bone) spurs, and can range from mildly unpleasant to very painful. The condition is usually caused from particularly high or low arches, and results in the tough underside of the foot (ligaments and tendons) being stretched and pulled away from the heel. Fasciitis can also be caused by overtraining, and/or having weak calves.

Shoes without enough midsole or arch support can exacerbate the condition, but are not usually the sole (no pun intended) cause.

Treatments:

- P.F. is caused over time, and the only remedy is time. You can help to prevent this injury by strengthening/stretching the calf muscles— by doing toe raises, or lying on your back and spelling out the letters of the alphabet with your toes. (These exercises are good for general strength and flexibility of the foot/calf area, and are good for shin splints as well.)

- Stay off of your feet as much as possible. If you're unable to give your feet a good 4-6 week vacation, then a cold heat regimen in the evenings and mornings helps promote healing: take a large metal can, glass jar, or ceramic cup without a handle, fill it with water and put it in the freezer. Roll the object back and forth under the arch and afflicted area of your foot for about 10 minutes. Then place your foot in a warm-water footbath for ten minutes. Keep trading back and forth until your ice is creating a big mess on the floor. The cold promotes decreased swelling and the release of inflammatories, while the warmth helps the tendons in the foot to relax.

- Look into an orthotic shoe insert that has good arch support and heel cushion. Heel cups have been reported to be successful also. If the condition is persistent and painful, consult a specialist who will be able to build an orthotic specifically for you.

Conditions:

You may have to stop running for a bit and switch to a stationary cycle or swimming to reduce the stress and strain on your feet. Stretching and massaging the undersides of your feet at least twice a day, and especially after exercising, will help dramatically, but the only sure way to heal is to allow time for your feet to recover. As a very last resort, there are cortisone shots that will reduce the inflammation of the tendons to help relieve pain, but this doesn't help to fix the biomechanical causes of the condition and could, in fact, worsen the it by persuading a person to do more than he or she is ready to do.

Hamstring and Achilles Tendon Strains and Pulls[12]

Symptoms:

Runners, trainers and coaches like to argue about what causes hamstring troubles—too flexible, not flexible enough, tight muscles, too-strong muscles—but the fact remains that the hamstring, which goes along the back of our legs and knees, does *a lot* of work when we run and exercise, and so is simply prone to soreness and injury. Hamstring issues are often persistent and may start with a twinge and soreness and, sometimes months or years later, suddenly become much worse. You will know immediately if your hamstring "goes out." The pain usually starts in the upper leg near the glutes, but then worsens down the back side of the leg if not given proper rest. For hamstring strains it's better to immediately give it rest rather than "run through it," as we will often favor the tender leg which causes an imbalanced running form, and even more trouble down the road.

Treatments:

- First, address the pain and swelling through rest, ice, compression, and anti-inflammatory medication in moderation.

- To begin rehab, start with stretching after warming the muscle in the shower or with a warm towel. Be gentle and remember movement-based stretching is more beneficial than static stretching.

- To strengthen the hamstrings, start with standing and prone leg curls: bend one knee to 90 (or as far as is possible) and hold for 10 seconds. Work both legs and build up to three sets of 10 repetitions, then add weights when you can proceed without pain. Use the back of a chair for balance, remembering to keep the back straight. Don't resume running until full strength and flexibility are regained.

- "Air squats" are also a great way to rebuild strength: with your feet shoulder-length apart, keep your eyes to the ceiling and squat until your thighs are at a 90 degree angle.

- If the condition persists, you may have to seek the help of a qualified physical therapist; a hamstring pull, if not taken care of, can keep us from running for months or even years.

Conditions:

There really is no good way to deal with a tender hamstring except by resting it. We want to be preventative and proactive with all soreness that might lead to injury, but with hamstrings and Achilles tendons we want to be extra cautious. We need to find alternative exercises to help strengthen the afflicted areas, and be very generous in our stretching and ice/heat regimes. Missing a race or workout is a small price to pay in comparison to the months of training we might lose in damaging these two vital areas.

Shin Splints[13]

Symptoms:

This is yet another condition that can range from uncomfortable to very painful. Aching and soreness start just behind the lower leg (tibia) and can worsen to acute pain as tendons start to pull away from the bone. Shin splints is a general term for lower leg problems, and occasionally is mistaken for a stress or hairline fracture of the tibia. The way to differentiate between the problems is that shin splint pain is somewhat alleviated through ice, blood-thinning pain relievers and rest, while stress or hairline fractures are not. The cause of shin splints is almost always the common cause of overuse on unforgiving surfaces—too much heel strike on concrete, asphalt and hard pack.

Treatments:

- At best, shin splints won't get better and at worst, you'll be setting the stage for a more serious injury. At the first symptoms of shin splints, stay off your feet, or at the very least, decrease your running time and/or distance.

- As with all of the injuries listed here, ice is the treatment of choice for reducing the inflammation, and shin splints are no exception. Massage shins with water that's been frozen in a foam or paper cup for 10 minutes at a time, up to four times a day for a week or two. You can also try icing shins splints with a bag of frozen vegetables. (Always remember, though, to use a cloth or paper towel between frozen materials and your skin.)

- Taping up your shin with an Ace bandage or with a neoprene sleeve that fits over the lower leg may be comforting for shin splints, because it compresses the muscles and permits less muscle movement. If this doesn't help with the ache in your lower leg, and you still feel a sharp pain, it's a strong indication of a stress or hairline fracture. (A stress fracture is a group of tiny fractures, usually in the lower leg or foot. A hairline fracture can be just as it sounds—a tiny crack in the bone. These are usually caused by overtraining, and occasionally caused by too-tight tendons pulling small chunks of bone out from where the tendons are anchored. You will know if you have a stress or hairline fracture by the large degree of pain, versus a sharp ache with shin splints.)

- Get off your feet, and if that's not possible, get off of the asphalt and concrete.

- Try orthotics.   More padding, in the midsole especially, may help to relieve some of the stress in the lower leg area.

Conditions:

Some people run and exercise with shin splints for years, while others find it completely debilitating. As with almost all other lower leg problems, we need to look closely at our form to see if over-pronating might be the cause, and be continually stretching and building the strength of our calves. As mentioned above, spelling out the alphabet with the toes is one of the best ways to strengthen the interconnected musculature of the calf/heel area.

Common Injury and Treatment Summary

- Having good, balanced core strength and good form is the best prevention of injury.

- Ice massages combined with warm heat are good for practically all soreness and injuries. Remember not to use extreme heat, or to place ice directly on the skin.

- Experiment with different orthotics, heel cups, or arch supports on short runs of low intensity.

- There is no surefire cure to any running injury except rest and a close inspection of underlying causes that may have contributed to the injured/sore area.

Visualization #3

It's 5 A.M. Cold, windy, and dark outside, but you're excited, and determined, because this is your time of day. You dress quietly with some extra precaution for the weather and head outside. There's no one else around, very few cars on the road, no lights on in the neighborhood.

As you finish your warm-ups and start down the road you feel an inordinate amount of pride in knowing that you are one of the few people awake at this hour; one of the very few out running in this weather. You think back to a month or so ago when you couldn't have imagined being up this early, let alone exercising at this hour. And actually enjoying it!

The wind is cold, and the footing underneath is a little slick, but you feel strong and confident as you continue on your run. You resist the urge to pick up the pace, knowing that the footing and weather are not a good combination for speed. Instead, you decide to take the loop that adds an extra mile to your run, enjoying your own steady pace, easy breathing, and the quiet morning.

When you return home, it strikes you that you just ran an extra mile at 5 in the morning with no hesitation at all.

You feel ready to greet the day and all its challenges.

Chapter 8: Running Inspired

Inspiration

If the key to running inspired could be summarized, it would be: Have Faith. Have enough faith in yourself to know that if you made it this far in the book and pursued the goal of running thus far, then getting out on the road and sticking with it will be no problem. If you've made it this far then getting out and running a few miles should be easy!

What is wonderful about running is that it is completely under our control. There are no gears, helmets, poles, clips, bindings, or other mechanical trappings to buy and fuss with. Running is only us and the trail or road, and the faith that what we are doing will bring its own rewards in time. We are in charge of how complicated or simple we make it, how we treat our bodies in the time between runs, and ultimately our entire attitude toward running. This can make running a little daunting, but, again, when we have faith in ourselves we change the mindset from, "This program better work!" to "I'm doing something wonderful for my mind and body, and I'm going to stick with it and let the results take care of themselves!" then wonderful things begin to happen, and we begin to run inspired.

There are hundred-and-one programs out there that all promise results, and they will all have some followers who find something in a program that works for them. Successful runners, though, and by successful we mean the ones who have run for years and still enjoy running, are the folks who have kept their running simple. They take care of their bodies, and they run consistently. No matter what the weather, time, or location, successful runners take the time to run.

We could call this dedication, but people are dedicated to their jobs, their families, to paying their mortgages . . . dedication implies a duty or act that *must* be performed. After running for a while we *will* find faith that running brings with it a certain freedom and inspiration that a gym, elliptical machine, or treadmill can't even come close to.

Finding support for you while you are a beginner runner in the form of a mentor, running club or online forum is a great way to get questions answered and to keep motivated. In the end, though, it's up to us to get up off of the couch and get running. This is why it is so important to listen to and take advice, yet at the same time make your running routine completely yours. Have rituals associated with your running that you enjoy. Create short and long-term goals that tie into your community, but are very important to you personally. Use your running time to think about your form, breathing and the next hill instead of dishes, bills and the next project deadline. Or conversely, use your running time as your mobile office to get the space and quiet for the quality thinking time so difficult to find elsewhere.

Your running methodology and motivations for running will change over time. That's okay. We want to be consistent only in that we run consistently. Otherwise, we want to trust our intuition to know when we can start pushing a little harder, when to let our bodies heal, what nutrients we need and don't need to stay healthy . . . mentors, coaches, specialized running programs, and personal trainers are great, but once we start having faith in our own intuition we essentially say that *we* are in charge of our own fitness and take pride in that fact.

At the point where we have confidence and pride in our own running program we discover that we stop running for results, or running because we need to, or have to, but because we want to. Because we know we'll feel better after a good run, because it's good for us physically and mentally, and because we're better able to help others when we take care of ourselves.

Whatever your size, shape, countenance or demeanor, no matter how much or how little fat jiggles as you jog, there is a running program that's just right for you. All you have to do to find that perfect program is have faith, keep it simple, trust your own intuition, and keep running. When you do these things consistently, you will undoubtedly run inspired.

And once you've become inspired, only you can set the limits of what you'll accomplish.

Chapter 9: Training Schedules

Training Schedule for Active Beginner Runners

If you already lead an active lifestyle, running is a great way to improve your overall fitness and endurance. This program is recommended for those who already run or exercise (such as walking, team sports, tennis, or swimming) at least a couple times per week, but want to expand their running/fitness regimen. It's also for those who are active, but need an exercise schedule to stay motivated. This plan will enable you to run 60 minutes at a decent pace and, upon completion, run a 5k or 10k race.

Training Schedule for Active Beginner Runners							
R = Run(ning) EP = Easy Pace	W = Walk(ing) MP = Moderate Pace		RJ = Run / Jog FP = Fast Pace		M = Minute(s) R+ = Rest		
Week #	Mon	Tue	Wed	Thu	Fri	Sat	Sun
Week 1	R 15 M at EP.	Alternate R 5 M at EP and 5 M at MP for 20 M.	Off	R 15 M at EP.	R 20 M at EP.	R 5 M at EP, followed by 5 M at FP. R+ 5 M. Repeat 3 times.	Off
Week 2	R 20 M at EP.	R 5 M at EP, 5 M MP, 5 M at EP, and 2 M at FP.	Off	R 10 M at EP, 10 M at MP.	R 20 M at EP.	R 10 M at EP, 10 M at MP. R+ 5 M. R3 M at FP.	Off
Week 3	R 20 M at EP.	R 5 M at EP, 10 M at MP, 10 M at EP.	Off	R 15 M at EP, 5 M at MP, 5 M at FP.	R 25 M at EP.	Alternate R 5 M at EP with 2 M at FP for 21 M	Off
Week 4	R 20 M at EP.	R 10 M at MP, 10 M at EP.	R 25 M at EP.	Off	R 20 M at EP.	R 10 M at MP, 2 M at FP, 5 M at EP, 10 M at MP.	Off
Week 5	R 30 M at EP.	Off	R 10 M at MP, 10 M at EP, 10 M at MP.	R 30 M at EP.	R 10 M at EP, 5 M at FP. R+ 2 M. Repeat twice.	R 35 M at EP.	Off
Week 6	R 30 M at EP.	R 10 M at MP, 2 M at EP, 15 M at MP.	R 20 M at EP.	Off	R 15 M at MP, 20 M at EP.	R 30 M at MP.	Off
Week 7	R 10 M at MP, 5 M at FP, 15 M at EP.	R 35 M at EP.	Off	R 20 M at EP, 10 M at MP.	R 25 M at EP.	R 10 M at MP, 2 M at FP. R+ 2 M. Repeat 3 times.	Off

Week 8	R 35 M at EP.	R 15 M at EP, 5 M at FP, 10 M at EP.	R 20 M at EP, 15 M at MP.	Off	R 20 M at EP, 5 M at FP.	R 10 M at MP, 5 M at FP, 5 M at EP. R+ 5 M. Repeat once.	Off
Week 9	R 20 M at EP.	R 10 M at MP, 5 M at FP, 5 M at EP. R+ 5 M. Repeat once.	R 30 M at EP.	Off	R 10 M at EP, 10 M at MP, 5 M at EP, 5 M at FP.	R 45 M at EP.	Off
Week 10	Alternate R 5 M at EP with 5 M at FP for 40 M.	Off	R 35 M at EP.	R 10 M at EP, 10 M at MP. R+ 5 M. Repeat once.	R 20 M at EP.	R 40 M at EP.	Off
Week 11	R 40 M at EP.	R 20 M at EP, 5 M at FP, 20 M at EP.	Off	R 30 M at EP.	R 10 M at EP, 20 at MP, 10 M at FP.	R 45 M at EP.	Off
Week 12	R 50 M at EP.	Off	Alternate R 10 M at EP with 5 M at FP for 40 M.	R 35 M at EP.	R 10 M at EP, 5 M at FP, 10 M at EP.	R 50 M at EP.	Off
Week 13	R 40 M at EP.	R 5 M at EP, 5 M at MP, 5 M at FP. R+ 5 M. Repeat once.	R 30 M at EP.	Off	R 20 M at MP.	R 55 M at EP.	Off
Week 14	R 20 M at MP.	R 10 M at EP, 5 M at FP, 5 M at EP. Repeat once.	R 25 M at MP.	R 30 M at EP.	Off	R 60 M at EP.	Off

* If you would prefer to take a different day off than the one scheduled, you can swap the day's workout with the off day. Just make sure you complete all five workouts each week.

** For all workouts, be sure to warm up and cool down with an easy 5 minutes of jogging.

*** For workouts that include repeats, don't rest unless it is specified.

Pace Key

Easy – Able to run and still carry on a conversation.

Moderate – Difficult to talk and run, but not impossible.

Fast – Run as fast as possible.

Training Schedule for Non-Exercisers

If you're looking for a way to kick your couch-potato ways and get into shape, running is an easy way to get active. This program is recommended for those who don't have a regular exercise regimen, but want to improve their fitness, lose a few pounds, and lead a more active lifestyle. This plan provides you with the proper training to eventually run (yes, run -- not jog!) for 60 minutes at a comfortable pace.

Training Schedule for Non-Exercisers							
R = Run(ning) W = Walk(ing) RJ = Run / Jog M = Minute(s)							
EP = Easy Pace MP = Moderate Pace FP = Fast Pace R+ = Rest							
Week #	Mon	Tue	Wed	Thu	Fri	Sat	Sun
Week 1	Alternate R 1 M at EP and W for 1 M for a total of 15 M.	R/J 10 M at an EP.	Off	Alternate R for 1 M at EP and W for 1 M for a total of 15 M.	R/J at an EP for 5 M, W 5 M. R+ 5 M. RJ 5 M at EP.	Run 15 M at EP.	Off
Week 2	R/J 10 M at EP.	W 5 M, R 5 M at EP. R+ 2 M. Repeat once.	Off	R 15 M at EP.	Alternate W for 1 M and R at EP for 1 M for a total of 20 M.	R/J 16 M at EP.	Off
Week 3	R 10 M at EP, R+ 5 M, R 10 M at EP.	R/J 15 M at EP.	R 5 M at EP, W 2 M, R/J 10 M at EP.	Off	R/J 15 M at EP.	Run 10 M at MP. R+ 5 M. R 10 M at EP.	Off
Week 4	R/J 17 M at EP.	R/J 10 M at EP, 5 M at MP, 2 M at FP.	Run 10 M at EP, W 5 M, R 10 M at EP.	Run 15 M at EP.	Off	Run 20 M at EP.	Off
Week 5	R 10 M at MP, 5 M at EP, 3 M at FP.	R/J 20 M at EP.	Off	R 5 M at EP, 2 M at FP. R+ 5 M. Repeat once.	R 15 M at EP.	R/J 25 M at EP.	Off
Week 6	R 16 M at EP.	R 5 M at MP, 5 M at EP. R+ 2 M. Repeat once	R/J 20 M at EP.	Off	R 15 M at EP, 5 M at MP.	R 27 M at EP.	Off
Week 7	R 10 M at EP, 5 M at MP, 5 M at EP.	R 15 M at EP, 5 M at MP, 2 M at FP.	Off	R 20 M at EP.	R 10 M at MP. R+ 5 M. R 5 M at FP, 5 M at EP.	R 30 M at EP.	Off
Week 8	R 20 M at EP.	R 10 M at MP, 10 M at EP. R+ 5 M. Repeat once.	R 25 M at EP.	Off	R 5 M at EP, 5 M at FP, 10 M at EP.	Alternate R 5 M at EP with 5 minutes at MP for 30 M.	Off

Week 9	R 25 M at EP.	R 10 M at MP, 5 M at EP, 5 M at FP.	Off	Alternate R 2 M at MP with 2 M at EP for 30 M.	R 10 M at EP, 10 M at MP.	R 35 M at EP.	Off
Week 10	R 30 M at EP.	R 5 M at MP, 5 M at EP, 3 M at FP. R+ 5 M. Repeat once.	Off	R 20 M at EP, 10 M at MP, 10 M at EP.	R 5 M at EP, 5 M at MP, 10 M at EP.	R 30 M at EP, 5 M at FP.	Off
Week 11	R 20 M at EP, 15 M at MP, 5 M at EP.	Alternate R 5 M at EP with 3 M at FP for 24 M.	Off	R 5 M at EP, 5 M at FP. R+ 2 M. Repeat 3 times.	R 25 M at EP.	R 40 M at EP.	Off
Week 12	R 35 M at EP.	R 15 M at MP, 5 M at EP, 10 M at MP.	Off	R 15 M at EP, 2 M at FP, 5 M at MP. R+ 5 M. Repeat once.	R 25 M at EP.	R 10 M at EP, 5 M at MP, 5 M at EP, 2 M at FP. R+ 2 M. Repeat once.	Off
Week 13	R 40 M at EP.	Off	R 10 M at EP, 5 M at FP, 10 M at EP, 10 M at MP.	R 15 M at EP, 15 M at EP.	R 20 M at EP.	R 50 M at EP.	Off
Week 14	R 45 M at EP.	R 10 M at EP, 5 M at MP, 10 M at EP, 5 M at FP.	Alternate R 5 M at EP with 1 M at FP for 42 minutes.	Off	R 20 M at EP, 10 M at MP, 15 M at EP.	R 20 M at EP.	Off
Week 15	R 40 M at EP.	R 10 M at EP, 5 M at FP. R+ 2 M. Repeat once.	R 25 M at EP, 10 M at MPv.	R 20 M at EP, 5 minutes at MP, 20 M at EP.	Off	R 60 M at EP.	Off

* If you would prefer to take a different day off than the one scheduled, you can swap the day's workout with the off day. Just make sure you complete all five workouts each week.

** For all workouts, be sure to warm up and cool down with an easy 5 minutes of jogging.

*** For workouts that include repeats, don't rest unless it is specified.

Pace Key

Jog – Faster than a walk, but not quite a run, either. A jog is more of a quick shuffling of the feet.

Jog/Run – For these workouts, try to run but if you're out of breath or struggling you can jog until you feel better.

Easy – Able to run and still carry on a conversation.

Moderate – Difficult to talk and run, but not impossible.

Fast – Run as fast as possible.

Training Schedule for Weight Loss

If you're overweight and need a way to lose the excess pounds, running may seem like an overly ambitious way to start, but it's actually a perfect weight-loss strategy. This program is recommended for those who are focusing on weight loss and want to start leading a healthier lifestyle. This plan provides the proper training to eventually run for 60 minutes at a comfortable pace. (Note: Before beginning any weight-loss exercise plan, you should check with your doctor to make sure you're healthy enough for physical activity.)

Training Schedule for Weight Loss							
R = Run(ning) J = Jog(ging) W = Walk(ing) RJ = Run / Jog M = Minute(s) EP = Easy Pace MP = Moderate Pace FP = Fast Pace R+ = Rest							
Week #	Mon	Tue	Wed	Thu	Fri	Sat	Sun
Week 1	W 5 M.	Off	W for 5 M, J for 1 M.	Off	W 10 M.	W 10 M, J 1 M.	Off
Week 2	W 10 M, J 2 M.	W 5 M, J 3 M.	Off	W 10 M, J 3 M.	Off	W 5 M, J 3 M, W 5 M.	Off
Week 3	J 10 M. R+ 5 M. R 1 M at EP.	J 10 M, W 5 M.	Off	J 10 M, W 5 M, R 2 M at EP.	Off	J 10 M, R 4 M at EP.	Off
Week 4	Alternate J 1 M with R 1 M at an EP for 15 M.	Off	J 5 M, R 10 M at EP, J 5 M.	Off	R 5 M at EP, J 5 M, R 1 M at MP.	R 10 M at EP, J 5 M.	Off
Week 5	R/J 10 M at EP.	J 5 M, R 5 M at EP, J 5 M, R 1 M at FP.	Off	R/J at EP for 15 M.	R 1 M at EP, 1 M at MP, J 5 M. R+ 2 M. Repeat once.	Alternate R 1 M at EP with 1 M J for 20 M.	Off
Week 6	R 15 M at EP.	R 5 M at EP, 2 M at MP. R+ 1 M. Repeat twice.	R 10 M at an EP. R+ 1 M. R/J 10 M at EP.	Off	Alternate R 2 M at EP with 2 M J for 26 M	R 20 M at EP.	Off
Week 7	R/J 18 M at EP.	R 7 M at EP, 2 M at FP, 1 M at EP. R+ 2 M. Repeat once.	Off	R 20 M at EP.	J 5 M, R 5 M at MP, R 10 M at EP.	R 1 M at MP, 1 M at FP, 2 M at EP. R+ 1 M. Repeat 5 times.	Off
Week 8	R 20 M at EP.	J 5 M, R 10 M at EP, J 5 M. R+ 1 M. R 5 M at MP.	R/J 25 M at EP.	R 10 M at EP, 2 M at FP, 10 M at EP, 2 M at FP.	Off	R 30 M at EP.	Off
Week 8	J 5 M, R 15 M at EP, J 5 M, R 5 M at MP.	R 22 M at EP.	Off	R 10 M at EP, 5 M at MP. R+ 5 M. Repeat once.	Alternate R 2 M at EP with 1 M at FP for 20 M.	R 5 M at EP, J 1 M. R+ 2 M. Repeat 5 times.	Off

Week 9	J 5 M, R 15 M at EP, J 5 M, R 5 M at MP.	R 22 M at EP.	Off	R 10 M at EP, 5 M at MP. R+ 5 M. Repeat once.	Alternate R 2 M at EP with 1 M at FP for 20 M.	R 5 M at EP, J 1 M. R+ 2 M. Repeat 5 times.	Off
Week 10	R 15 M EP.	J 5 M, R 10 M at EP, J 5 M at EP.	R 20 M at EP.	Off	Alternate R 2 M at EP with 2 M of J for 30 M.	R 20 M at EP, R 2 M at FP.	Off
Week 11	R/J 20 M at EP.	R 10 M at EP, 5 M at MP, 15 M at EP.	Off	R 20 M at EP.	J 15 M, R 5 M at EP, R 2 M at MP.	R 35 M at EP.	Off
Week 12	R 20 M at EP.	Alternate R 5 M at EP, with 2 M at FP for 21 M.	Off	J 10 M, R 15 M at EP, J 5 M.	J 15 M.	R 40 M at EP.	Off
Week 13	R 30 M at EP.	R 15 M at EP, 5 M at MP.	R 10 M at EP, 3 M at MP, 2 M at EP. Rest 5 M. Repeat once.	Off	J 5 M, R 15 M at EP.	R 20 M at EP, J 5 M, R 20 M at EP.	Off
Week 14	R 25 M at EP.	Off	R 10 M at EP, J 10 M, R 10 M at EP.	Off	R 20 M at EP.	R 50 M at EP.	Off
Week 15	R 30 M at EP.	Alternate R 5 M at EP with 1 M at FP for 24 M.	R 15 M at EP, J 5 M.	R 20 M at EP.	Off	R 25 M at EP, 10 M at MP, 15 M at EP, 5 M at MP.	Off
Week 16	R 30 M at EP.	R 15 M at EP, J 5 M, R 15 M at MP.	R 15 M at EP, 5 M at FP.	R 20 M at EP.	Off	R 60 M at EP. (Don't jog! You can do this!)	Off

* If you would prefer to take a different day off than the one scheduled, you can swap the day's workout with the off day. Just make sure you complete all five workouts each week.

** For all workouts, be sure to warm up and cool down with an easy 5 minutes of walking or jogging.

*** For workouts that include repeats, don't rest unless it is specified.

Pace Key

Jog – Faster than a walk, but not quite a run, either. A jog is more of a quick shuffling of the feet.

Jog/Run – For these workouts, try to run but if you're out of breath or struggling you can jog until you feel better.

Easy – Able to run and still carry on a conversation.

Moderate – Difficult to talk and run, but not impossible.

Fast – Run as fast as possible.

Training Schedule for People 50 and Older

If you're 50 or older, staying active is extremely important to maintaining good health and running is an easy and fun way to stay fit. This program is recommended for those who are 50 or older and want to lose a few pounds or run to maintain a healthy lifestyle. This plan provides the proper training that will enable you to run for 60 minutes at a comfortable pace. (Note: Before beginning any exercise plan, you should check with your doctor to make sure you're healthy enough for physical activity.)

Training Schedule for People 50 and Older							
R = Run(ning) J = Jog(ging) W = Walk(ing) RJ = Run / Jog M = Minute(s) EP = Easy Pace MP = Moderate Pace FP = Fast Pace R+ = Rest							
Week #	Mon	Tue	Wed	Thu	Fri	Sat	Sun
Week 1	R/J 5 M at an EP. W 5 M.	Off	R/J 8 M at EP, R 2 M at FP.	R 5 M at EP, J 5 M.	R 5 M at EP, J 5 M.	R 6 M at EP, J 6 M.	Off
Week 2	R/J 10 M at EP, R 3 M at MP.	R 15 M at EP.	Off	R 8 M at EP, 2 M at FP.	Off	Alternate R 1 M at MP with 1 M at EP for 12 M.	Off
Week 3	R/J 13 M at EP. R+ 2 M. R 2 M at MP.	Off	Alternate R 1 M at EP with 1 M of J for 15 M.	Off	R/J 15 M at EP.	R 10 M at EP, J 5 M, R 5 M at EP.	Off
Week 4	R 15 M at EP.	R 10 M at EP, 5 M at MP, 5 M at EP.	Off	R 3 M at MP, 3 M at EP, 3 M at FP. R+ 5 M. Repeat once.	R 10 M at EP.	R 10 M at EP, 2 M at MP, 10 M at EP.	Off
Week 5	R 18 M at EP.	R 5 M at MP, 2 M at FP. R+ 2 M. Repeat once.	R 15 M at EP, 3 M at MP.	Off	R 15 M at EP.	Alternate R 2 M at EP with 1 M at MP for 24 M.	Off
Week 6	R 20 M at EP.	R 10 M at EP, 5 M at MP, 10 M at EP.	Off	R 5 M at MP, 10 M at EP, 2 M at FP.	Off	R 30 M at EP.	Off
Week 7	R 20 M at EP.	R 10 M at EP, J 5 M, R 10 M at MP.	Off	R 5 M at EP, 5 M at MP, 10 M at EP.	R 15 M at EP.	R 20 M at EP. R+ 5 M. R 15 M at EP.	Off
Week 8	R 10 M at EP, 2 M at FP, 5 M at EP.	Off	Alternate R 1 M at EP with 1 M, J for 25 M.	Off	R 10 M at EP, 2 M at FP, 8 M at EP.	R 40 M at EP.	Off
Week 8	R 25 M at EP.	R 15 M at EP, 5 M at MP.	Alternate R 5 M at EP with 1 M FP for 24 M.	Off	R 15 M at EP.	R 10 M at EP, 5 M at MP. R+ 5 M. Repeat twice.	Off

Week 9	R 25 M at EP.	R 15 M at EP, 5 M at MP.	Alternate R 5 M at EP with 1 M FP for 24 M.	Off	R 15 M at EP.	R 10 M at EP, 5 M at MP. R+ 5 M. Repeat twice.	Off
Week 10	R 15 M at EP, 10 M at MP.	Off	R 5 M at EP, 1 M at FP. R+ 2 M. Repeat 3 times.	Off	R 20 M at EP.	R 45 M at EP.	Off
Week 11	R 5 M at EP, 10 M at MP, J 5 M.	R 25 M at EP.	Off	R 10 M at EP, 3 M at FP. R+ 5 M. Repeat once.	R/J 30 M at EP.	R 10 M at EP, 10 M at MP, 2 M at EP, 3 M at FP.	Off
Week 12	R 10 M at EP, 5 M at FP, 10 M at EP.	Off	R/J 10 M, R 5 M at MP, R 15 M at EP.	R 15 M at EP.	Off	R 50 M at EP.	Off
Week 13	R 20 M at EP.	R/J 10 M at EP, R 4 M at MP. R+ 5 M. Repeat once.	R 15 M at EP, 5 M at MP, 2 M at FP.	Off	R/J 20 M at EP.	R 10 M at MP, 5 M at EP, 2 M at FP. R+ 2 M. Repeat once.	Off
Week 14	R 40 M at EP.	R 20 M at EP, 5 M at FP.	Off	R 10 M at EP, 15 M at MP.	Off	R 20 M at EP, 10 M at MP. R+ 5 M. R 15 M at EP.	Off
Week 15	R 20 M at EP.	R 10 M at MP, 5 M at EP, 2 M at FP.	Off	R 25 M at EP.	Off	R 60 M at EP.	Off

* If you would prefer to take a different day off than the one scheduled, you can swap the day's workout with the off day. Just make sure you complete all five workouts each week.

** For all workouts, be sure to warm up and cool down with an easy 5 minutes of walking or jogging.

*** For workouts that include repeats, don't rest unless it is specified.

Pace Key

Jog – Faster than a walk, but not quite a run, either. A jog is more of a quick shuffling of the feet.

Jog/Run – For these workouts, try to run but if you're out of breath or struggling you can jog until you feel better.

Easy – Able to run and still carry on a conversation.

Moderate – Difficult to talk and run, but not impossible.

Fast – Run as fast as possible.

Free Downloadable PDF Running Schedule Downloads: Four Specialized Schedules to Help You Get Started

Why download the training schedules?

These specialized training schedules target specific people: people who are already active, people who haven't been active in awhile, beginning runners who want to lose weight and a schedule for those age 50 and up.

By downloading the schedules, you can print them out and take them anywhere, write your own notes and reminders on them, and truly make them yours! I invite you to truly engage in the schedule that fits you best and let me know how it works for you. Downloading the schedule that fits you best is like having your own personal running coach with you anywhere, any time.

What is the download?

The schedules are downloaded in a simple, easy to use PDF format. Download the schedules and print out as much or as little as you'd like to help give your initial runs focus and direction.

How do I download the running schedules?

Go to **thekeytorunning.com** and fill in your name, email address and receipt number from Amazon to receive the download link. If you do not have a receipt number, you may enter the words "Running Inspired" instead. (omit the quotation marks).

I promise that your email will *not* be sold to any third parties, and will only be used to notify you of any new books, or share important running information identified by readers. You can opt out of the mail list at any time, but I think you will find the information and sharing of knowledge invaluable.

About the Author

Ryan Robert grew up in western Oregon playing football, basketball, baseball, and running track when time allowed.

During and after college he became an avid runner, and coached cross-country runners while teaching. Ryan really became educated about running, though, while working with and training firefighters for the Forest Service--one of the most physically demanding jobs there is.

It was during this period that he developed the training that creates not only a good runner, but someone who is well-rounded, healthy, and strong.

Ryan currently runs and skis in the Alaska back country, where he constantly refines his writing and running. Although he doesn't race competitively, he is always trying to improve form and technique, for himself and a few select runners and skiers who seek him as a coach and mentor.

Inspired? Or Uninspired? Please let me know what you thought of the book by leaving a review.

Thank you so much for reading *Running Inspired*. I encourage you to share your newfound knowledge with other runners who might be tentative, scared or in need of support in starting their own running journey.

In this same spirit, I have received valuable criticism, praise, and questions from readers all over the world. Please help me to make this the best book it can be by leaving me a review on Amazon. Runners won't always agree on everything, but hopefully together we can get more people out there running and engaging in the debate!

Sincerely,
Ryan J. Robert

References:

1.   Laukkanen, Jari A.; Laaksonen, David E.; Niskamen, Leo; Hakkarainen, Anna; Salonen, Jukka T. 2004. "Metabolic Syndrome and the Risk of Prostate Cancer in Finnish Men: A population-Based study." *Cancer Epidemiology, Biomarkers & Prevention.* 13;1646.

2.   Benjamin, Mike. 2009. "The Fascia of the Limbs and Back: A Review". *Journal of Anatomy.* 214(1): 1–18.

3.   Wilmore, Jack H.; Costill, David L.; 2004. "Physiology of Sport and Exercise: third edition". *Human Kinetics.* p.100.

4,5,6,7,8.   Wilmore, Jack H.; Costill, David L.; 2004. "Physiology of Sport and Exercise: third edition". *Human Kinetics.* p.279-282.

9.   Wilmore, Jack H.; Costill, David L.; 2004. "Physiology of Sport and Exercise: third edition". *Human Kinetics.* p.46-52.

10. William Prentice. 2003. "Arheim's Principles of Athletic Training: a Competency-based Approach." Eleventh Edition.*Mcgraw-Hill Higher Education.* p.613-614.

11.   William Prentice. 2003. "Arheim's Principles of Athletic

Training: a Competency-based Approach." Eleventh Edition. *Mcgraw-Hill Higher Education.* p.511-513.

12.   William Prentice. 2003. "Arheim's Principles of Athletic Training: a Competency-based Approach." Eleventh Edition. *Mcgraw-Hill Higher Education.* p. 549-551, 633-635.

13. William Prentice. 2003. "Arheim's Principles of Athletic Training: a Competency-based Approach." Eleventh Edition. *Mcgraw-Hill Higher Education.* p.555.

Made in the USA
Columbia, SC
18 February 2020

88124066R00076